Microcomputers for Financial Planning

Second edition

Rodney Drew and Geoff Smith
3i Consultants Limited

Gower

in association with

3i Consultants Limited

Published by
Gower Publishing Company Limited
Gower House
Croft Road
Aldershot
Hants   GU11 3HR
England

Gower Publishing Company
Old Post Road
Brookfield
Vermont 05036
U.S.A.

The authors wish to thank Planning Sciences Limited for their assistance with the section on 'MasterModeller'. The 'MasterModeller' copyright is held by Planning Sciences Limited and the copyright for 'Strategy Modeller' by 3i Consultants Limited.

British Library Cataloguing in Publication Data

Drew, Rodney
    Microcomputers for financial planning.—2nd ed.
    1. Business enterprises—Finance—Data processing
    I. Title   II. Smith, Geoff
    658.1'5'0285416   HG4012.5

Library of Congress Cataloging in Publication Data

Drew, Rodney
    Microcomputers for financial planning.
    Includes index.
    1. Business enterprises—Finance—Data processing.
    2. Corporations—Finance—Data processing.
    3. Microcomputers.   I. Smith, Geoff, 1926-
    II. Title.
    HG4012.5.D73   1987   658.1'5'0285416   87-8405

ISBN 0-566-02579-5

Printed in Great Britain by Henry Ling Ltd., at the Dorset Press, Dorchester, Dorset

Contents

APPENDICES

List of Figures

Introduction

Much has changed since the first edition of this book was written in the early 1980s. This is true for the business climate generally and the information industry in particular. In 1983 we wrote: 'Today's business climate is probably the most difficult and competitive that management can remember. The best that can be expected is that things may not get any worse'. Six years on, we can be more optimistic. Manufacturing output has reached its highest level for six years, and there are signs that unemployment may also be bottoming out, although manufacturing employment is still falling. Long-term forecasts vary, depending on their source, but, as in 1983, even the most optimistic indicate that the days of low interest rates and easy markets hungry for goods and services are a thing of the past. With foreign products taking an ever larger share of our markets, more than ever before there is a clear need for you to stay ahead of the game in every aspect of your business and to respond as early as possible to events that will affect the business and opportunities that may be presented to it. Even this type of approach, however, suffers from being essentially a reactive one - waiting for something to happen and then deciding upon the best course of action in the circumstances. It might have been adequate some years ago, but even then to be workable it needed to be based on the assumption that not too much would occur at once, so that the choice between the available options would be relatively simple and straightforward, and the necessary thinking not too convoluted. Perhaps the reality of what needs to be done for effective business planning has always been different, and what has been lacking is a usable aid to make the whole process feasible for the complex situation that actually exists, rather than in an artificially simplified form.

How many times have you heard an industrialist say: 'You can't forecast in this business', 'We have all our time cut out just keeping up with the competition' or 'It's as much as we can do to solve today's problems, let alone tomorrow's.'? This type of statement is then often followed by a circular argument which says that if you know you cannot forecast accurately, any plans you make will be worthless, any decisions based on the plans may well be defective, so you may as well not bother. Such companies, as it were, post a few lookouts, and steer the corporate ship by dead reckoning. Rather like the early navigators, they are therefore bound to keep in sight of land - closely in touch with the familiar ground on which the business has long operated.

The trouble is that this approach is visibly less effective day by day. The horizon is often obscured by fog, the weather changes regularly (usually from bad to worse) and many other vessels are ploughing our once exclusive routes. The old 'coaster' may be a romantic idea, but that is all that can be said of it.

You may be wondering : 'Are they now going to say that the whole of the problems of British industry - the fluctuating pound, foreign competition, wage settlements higher than inflation and the rest - can be solved by another piece of micro-technology?' Hardly. But the availability of inexpensive microcomputers can be harnessed to make efficient planning a practical reality in businesses of all sizes, even in an environment that changes so fast that plans have to be updated and recast very frequently.

None of these opening comments has in any way been specifically related to the use of microcomputers for planning. That is simply because their use in this area is both to automate and to extend the scope of planning - machines themselves are best regarded as aids to planning - rather than to engender an understanding of the reasons for planning itself, or how to go about it.

In this book, however, we look first at how conventional business planning systems operate, how they relate to the systems of accounting normally found in companies, and then isolate the defects and difficulties of manual planning methods. Computers are then considered as part of a solution to the planning problem, and a detailed description of a standard microcomputer planning program is used to show how to use and apply the techniques.

We are concerned here essentially with financial planning. This covers the evaluation of all aspects of the business, with the objective of forecasting profit, requirements for working capital, investment and so on. Marketing planning - that is everything directly related to the products or services on offer, such as pricing, discounts, gross margins, relative product and market profitability and the like - is a subject on its own and concerns us here only to the extent that forecasts made as part of the marketing planning process provide the base for the financial plan.

This book and its companion volumes have been conceived as practical down-to-earth guides. In the various chapters of Part I we shall be discussing business planning methods, the solutions offered by computers, and the standard planning software available. Part II is devoted to the technical aspects of microcomputers and contains advice on how to go about selecting appropriate equipment for your own requirements.

Part I

Chapter 1
BUSINESS PLANNING — AND THE LACK OF IT

Planning is often discussed as if it were the exclusive preserve of multi-national corporations. To do it at all, there is the underlying impression that there must at least be someone called 'Manager' - Corporate Planning' on the staff, possibly with one or two economists and business school graduates in attendance as well. In reality, nothing could be further from the truth. All businesses plan to a greater or lesser extent, even those that would deny it flatly if asked, including our local fish and chip shop! Although you would be most unlikely to spend much time discussing with the proprietor whether or not it was 'a well-planned business', you are doubtless aware of the results of the owner's planning - or lack of it! Just how long do you have to wait for chips?

Planning also has a bad name, if only because 'lack of planning' is so often cited as the reason for any problem or disaster, as if to infer that the whole planning process is either impossible or invariably bungled. Many managements claim that there is no point in planning because 'things change so often'. With conventional planning systems, this indeed creates a major difficulty, as plans committed to paper are obviously hard to revise without a complete rewrite every time they go out of date. In addition, they are usually compiled by people who have a great deal of regular day-to-day work to do as well - perhaps a firm's accountant and his staff. While an annual planning exercise may perhaps be coped with, the prospect of any regular revision of plans, let alone their regular complete rewriting in the face of changed circumstances, is almost universally resisted at the administrative level, even if supported by directors and managers above.

It is also undeniably true, however, that out-of-date plans are useless for any purpose other than that of judging how <u>wrong</u> things have gone. They immediately cease to have any part to play in the future of the business and the decision-making processes, the role for which they were presumably conceived in the first place.

It is this compound excuse - that of it being difficult to find the time for planning in the first place, the impossibility of reworking plans as things change, and their quickly becoming useless as they become more and more out of date - that leads to the decision (or tacit acceptance) in most businesses that explicit planning is not for them. Nevertheless, planning is still carried out implicitly in all those businesses. Each time a decision is made, various information is collected and considered, different options and opinions are discussed and eventually a conclusion is reached on what to do. Sometimes an attempt is made to predict the long-term consequences of decisions, but as they are being taken time after time and normally in isolation, this is extremely difficult, as the results of each decision tend to interact with the results of others, and the effects of all decisions are compounded into a tangled mess. The eventual results are always clear enough, but the reasons behind them are lost.

As far as taking the responsibility for what goes right or wrong is concerned, there could be managements who find this scenario acceptable, as it makes the identification of responsibility for what happens extremely difficult. Nevertheless, good planning, if the problems already described could be overcome, should be a positive aid to making things go right (or at least as required) most of the time, and reducing the need for witch hunts and recriminations.

Marketing Planning

In the same way as there is no requirement to have a 'corporate planning department' in order to do any business planning, there is no need for a marketing department to do marketing planning. The marketing process is often defined as:

'Identifying customer needs and satisfying them at a profit.'

If this is so, it includes a range of activities from, say, research, through product identification and design, to sales. Different groups of activities are taken to comprise 'marketing' in different companies, and their precise combination is not important here. What must be clear is that every company will already be taking many decisions in this area, even if only to be in a position to tell the factory what products to make and customers what price they will have to pay. Few businesses answer the customer's question 'How much is it?' with 'We haven't thought about it yet'. Equally obvious is the need for planning systems to be based on the marketing of whatever products or services the business may be engaged in.

Everything else in the business must logically relate to the prospect of sales being made and certain revenues and margins accruing from them. The days are long gone when it was a good idea to make whatever you chose and to hope people would want to buy it. Even companies engaging in huge amounts of research will, if they are to remain successful, try to relate their expenditure in this area directly to the amount of sales anticipated from the newly developed items.

To begin with, all marketing planning, whether done manually or by computer, will need to be related in some way to a range of data about the products (or services) themselves. Some of this data may come from the company's accounting system, which may, if sufficiently thorough, be able to provide details about the performance and profitability of each product separately. Other facts may be gathered from sales records, salesmen's reports and similar sources. Unfortunately such information is only going to tell us what has happened in the past, and will therefore provide only a part of what is needed to compile a reliable marketing plan. The remainder of the story must include data about the customers who buy or might buy the products together with judgements made by those responsible for obtaining sales on how many of their customers will actually buy, and, most importantly, what price they will be prepared to pay.

As an example let us look at how this process takes place in our own company, a management consultancy operating out of several regional centres, and with a few additional centrally managed activities as well.

Regional managers keep records of enquiries, proposals and sales, and receive monthly accountancy information on invoiced sales revenue, direct costs, overheads and contributions. All this is shown in relation to an annual budget in month and year-to-date formats. Half-yearly, a checklist of marketing activity being undertaken is completed, giving a picture of where and how effort is being directed to generate enquiries. Annually, regional managers are asked to submit forecasts of sales under a number of product categories, and these forecasts are consolidated at head office to give the first picture of expected sales revenue in the following financial year. The forecasts are based on the fee levels we intend to obtain for the various grades of professional staff used.

When described in a few words, it all sounds like a relatively straightforward process. It has not always been like that and in administrative terms, at least, still is not. Neither have we mentioned the very difficult process of deciding what services to offer, and when to phase out the old ones and bring in new developments. Our planning process is still evolving, and we are aware of a number of defects, but it has the central benefit, essential to all good marketing planning, that those responsible for marketing and for obtaining sales make the forecasts. Various developments over the last few years have aided our planning process, not the least being the implementation of computerised accounting and the recently improved analysis of information that we can now obtain.

Chapter 2
THE ROLE OF ACCOUNTING INFORMATION

The use of accounting information in planning is vital, and it is often through accounting and the efforts of the company accountants that the first planning steps are taken. Accountants probably call them 'budgets', and although there is endless argument about the differences and/or similarities between budgets and plans, suffice it to say that they are closely enough related to bear examination together and to be highly relevant to the subject under discussion.

Most well organised accounting systems will keep the records of a company's progress in financial terms in three main 'ledgers', supported by various other records, including cash books, day books and the like. The three ledgers record all the details about the company's sales and receipts, purchases and payments, and, in the 'general' or 'nominal' ledger, an analysis of the expenditure and income of the whole business. Where the company is divided into several cost and profit centres or trades as a set of subsidiaries under a holding company, these records will be equivalently sub-divided. Most larger companies, and an increasing number of smaller ones, produce a whole range of reports and analyses on a regular basis (normally monthly), which summarise progress in any number of ways and are used by management as the main method of monitoring what is happening to the business, and as the basis for deciding what to do if progress is not satisfactory. With the advent of low-cost microcomputers and cheap standard accounting software to run on them, even the smallest business can contemplate using an automated system and gaining the benefit of much improved analysis and control.

Figure 2.1, which shows a typical statement of monthly results and sales for a small manufacturing company, will be familiar to all accountants and many managers brought up on larger company systems. It is clear that, to compile the statement, a great deal of data has had to be collected and summarised. To achieve this, a comprehensive coding system for all items of income and expenditure must be operating, together with a relatively sophisticated costing system.

**Figure 2.1   XYZ Ltd - Four-weekly statement, Period 10,
4 weeks ended: Oct 7**

I Orders and sales	This Period	To Date
		This Year
	£	£
Orders received, less cancellations	15,000	187,125
Net sales	14,250	211,035
Orders on hand at close	54,000	54,000
II Revenue account		
Sales, net	14,250	211,105
	14,250	211,105
Prime cost of production (a)	8,250	101,250
less closing stocks and work-in-progress, plus opening stocks and work-in-progress	(1,800)	1,453
GROSS PROFIT	7,800	108,402
Operating expenses (b)	6,828	65,277
OPERATING PROFIT	972	43,125
Miscellaneous income	60	405
	1,032	43,530
Miscellaneous expenditure	534	4,692
NET PROFIT, subject to taxation and appropriation	498	38,838
NET PROFIT for year		
(a) Prime cost of production		
Labour	3,500	42,500
Materials	3,600	45,000
Direct charges	1,150	13,750
TOTAL	8,250	101,250
(b) Operating expenses		
Standing charges	1,275	12,750
Salaries and indirect labour	2,625	25,050
Other operating expenses	2,478	23,187
Depreciation	450	4,290
TOTAL	6,828	65,277

Budgets

One obvious defect of the statement in Figure 2.1 is that it only shows what has happened in the past and gives the reader no indication whether or not this is satisfactory in the circumstances or has any relation to what was expected to occur. Some companies choose to illuminate this area by a comparison with what happened at the same time last year, and Figure 2.2 shows an extended version of the company results in Figure 2.1, with this information added. Clearly, the results from this method are clouded by the effects of inflation, and the question immediately arises as to whether or not the 'improvement' shown amounts to anything significant in real terms. As an alternative, many companies choose to draw up budgets of what they expect to occur in the year to come and use these as the basis of comparison. The same analysis appears with budget comparisons in Figure 2.3.

For all practical purposes the existence of a budget for, say, the year ahead must be considered as some form of planning. As the year progresses, however, the period ahead for which budgets exist gets shorter and shorter, and so the planning horizon is constantly diminished. One eventually reaches the year-end with no plans at all!

Companies approach the construction of their plans and budgets in a variety of ways, of which the earlier example of the management consultancy was but one. In some, the accountants do most or all of the work, making judgements on the effect of inflation on sales, costs and so on, and thereby coming up with the next year's figures in what they would argue to be a realistic way. This has been found to be less than satisfactory for a number of reasons, the main one being the lack of commitment to achieve the figures by the various managers, as they have had nothing to do with their preparation. In addition, there is a great danger of the figures themselves being suspect, as the accountants may not know enough about such things as market and product changes, new production methods and so on, which may radically alter the likely trends of sales and costs. Clearly, the application of any automated techniques to a planning process done on this or any other unsatisfactory basis will in no way influence the acceptability or credibility of the figures, though it may reduce the accountants' workload.

A more enlightened approach is to provide the people responsible for various aspects of the business with adequate information on their area of responsibility in financial terms and thereafter obtain from them their estimates and judgements on what is likely to happen in the months and years to come. This is not to suggest that such data is then blindly incorporated into the plans and budgets without any consideration at all by the top management or financial people, but all plans should be rooted in such information if they are to be considered at all realistic. Examples drawn up in this way are shown in Figures 2.4 and 2.5. Further, if the genuine belief results that, although the views submitted are thought broadly believable, the consequent results are unsatisfactory, the need for decisions to be taken to make sufficient changes to produce acceptable results is revealed at the earliest moment.

This, then, is the main justification and reason for planning of any sort: the ability to predict results in the first place and take action early if the predictions reveal problems or difficulties associated with the course of action being contemplated.

With manual systems, however, the taking of such action is difficult. Even the simple operational budget in Figure 2.4 shows just how many areas there are in which changes could be made. Many of them have consequential effects on other areas. Therefore, while it is obviously necessary to show the effects of any

Figure 2.2   XYZ Ltd - Four-weekly statement, Period 10,
4 weeks ended: Oct 7

I Orders and sales	This Year	To Date	
		This Year	Last Year
	£	£	£
Orders received, less cancellations	15,000	187,125	211,278
Net sales	14,250	211,035	223,176
Orders on hand at close	54,000	54,000	71,922
II Revenue account			
Sales, net	14,250	211,105	220,472
	14,250	211,105	220,472
Prime cost of production (a)	8,250	101,250	113,979
less closing stocks and work-in-progress, plus opening stocks and work-in-progress	(1,800)	1,453	(2,290)
GROSS PROFIT	7,800	108,402	108,783
Operating expenses (b)	6,828	65,277	54,813
OPERATING PROFIT	972	43,125	53,970
Miscellaneous income	60	405	300
	1,032	43,530	54,270
Miscellaneous expenditure	534	4,692	2,616
NET PROFIT, subject to taxation and appropriation	498	38,838	51,654
NET PROFIT for year			58,000
(a) Prime cost of production			
Labour	3,500	42,500	48,175
Materials	3,600	45,000	48,796
Direct charges	1,150	13,750	17,008
TOTAL	8,250	101,250	113,979
(b) Operating expenses			
Standing charges	1,275	12,750	11,700
Salaries and indirect labour	2,625	25,050	23,895
Other operating expenses	2,478	23,187	15,168
Depreciation	450	4,290	4,050
TOTAL	6,828	65,277	54,813

**Figure 2.3   XYZ Ltd – Four-weekly statement, Period 10,
4 weeks ended: Oct 7**

I Orders and sales	This Period		To Date		
			This Year		Last Year
	Budget	Actual	Budget	Actual	Actual
	£	£	£	£	£
Orders received, less cancellations	20,000	15,000	200,000	187,125	211,278
Net sales	19,500	14,250	195,000	211,035	223,176
Orders on hand at close		54,000		54,000	71,922
II Revenue account					
Sales, net	19,500	14,250	195,000	211,105	220,472
		14,250		211,105	220,472
Prime cost of production (a)	8,000	8,250	80,000	101,250	113,979
Less closing stocks and work-in-progress, plus opening stocks and work-in-progress		(1,800)		1,453	(2,290)
GROSS PROFIT	11,500	7,800	115,000	108,402	108,783
Operating expenses (b)	6,000	6,828	60,000	65,277	54,813
OPERATING PROFIT	5,500	972	55,000	43,125	53,970
Miscellaneous income		60		405	300
		1,032		43,530	54,270
Miscellaneous expenditure		534		4,692	2,616
NET PROFIT, subject to taxation and appropriation	5,500	498	55,000	38,838	51,654
NET PROFIT for year			52,487		58,000
(a) Prime cost of production					
Labour	3,250	3,500	32,500	42,500	48,175
Materials	3,500	3,600	35,000	45,000	48,796
Direct charges	1,250	1,150	12,500	13,750	17,008
TOTAL	8,000	8,250	80,000	101,250	113,979
(b) Operating expenses					
Standing charges	550	1,275	5,500	12,750	11,700
Salaries and indirect labour	2,500	2,625	25,000	25,050	23,895
Other operating expenses	2,500	2,478	25,000	23,187	15,168
Depreciation	450	450	4,500	4,290	4,050
TOTAL	6,000	6,828	60,000	65,277	54,813

changes in a revised set of figures, and to keep on trying until acceptable results obtain, it will never be feasible to attempt manually to evaluate more than a small number of the available combinations of circumstances that might be brought about. Furthermore, when conclusions have been reached on what to do, there will always be the underlying worry that perhaps some other plan would have been better still, if only there had been time to work it all out.

Areas Where Changes Can Be Made

In order to illustrate these types of changes to plans, consider the sales director's budget shown in Figure 2.5 This is a more detailed breakdown of the sales side of the budget in the previous figure. Sales of three products are considered, each with different levels of profitability. In order to improve the position revealed in the budget, the following types of action might be considered:

(a)   cut manufacturing costs;
(b)   raise prices;
(c)   reduce discounts;
(d)   increase discounts (sell more)
(e)   reduce debtors (settlement discounts);
(f)   reduce distribution costs (minimum orders).

Each of the areas of reducing costs and increasing sales breaks down into a number of sub-areas, for example:

| Increasing Sales | - more or better quality advertising;
- better sales training;
- better conversion of quotations;
- better knowledge of the market. |
| Reducing Costs | - more process automation;
- less borrowing;
- better purchasing;
- less administration. |

Even this raises more and more variables. Take borrowing. The need for cash depends on the business's consumption of working capital. In approximate terms this comprises the company's investment in stocks of raw materials and finished goods, the costs of work-in-progress, the money owed by debtors less the money owed to creditors. It is in the cash flow of the business that the effect of these items is seen. A supposedly attractive option might be one of achieving increased sales, but it can easily be deduced that a much larger cash requirement (and therefore bank overdraft) might result, as debtors, creditors and stocks would have to rise to support the higher trading level. In times of high interest rates the extra interest repayments might well consume all the benefit of the increased sales, particularly if the margin on each extra item sold was relatively small.

Thus, the interrelation of all the effects of the different actions that might be taken in the planning and budgeting process is easy to demonstrate as being highly complex. And the reason for the often encountered reluctance to plan in the first place - or at least, replan at all frequently - is very clearly illustrated.

Figure 2.4   Operational budget reflecting departmental delegation of authority (£000s)

	Last Year Total	Total	Managing Director (Mr A)	Sales Director (Mr B)	Production Manager (Mr C)	Development Engineer (Mr D)	Chief Accountant (Mr E)	Secretary (Mr F)	Contra Items	Subsidiary Schedule No.
Sales:										
Manufactured - Home	3100.0	3100.0		3100.0						A
- Export	850.0	850.0		850.0						
Factored Sub-Total	3950.0	3950.0		3950.0						
- Home	190.0	190.0		190.0						
- Export	30.0	30.0		30.0						
Total	4170.0	4170.0		4170.0						
Stock adjustments										
Opening stocks	748.0	748.0	748.0							
Closing stocks	792.0	792.0	792.0							
Net	44.0	44.0	44.0							
Production & factored sales	4214.0	4214.0	44.0	4170.0	3994.0				(3994.0)	
Prime costs										
Direct labour	1467.0	1467.0			1467.0					
Materials	1133.0	1133.0			1133.0					
Cost of factored goods	70.0	70.0		70.0						
Total	2670.0	2670.0			2600.0					
Gross profit	1544.0	1544.0	44.0	4100.0	1394.0				(3994.0)	
Overhead expenses										
Works	226.0	226.0			226.0					B
Maintenance	36.8	36.8			36.8					C
Buying	17.5	17.5			17.5					D
Transport	24.3	24.3			24.3					E
Stores	30.6	30.6			30.6					F
Production engineering	22.5	22.5			22.5					G
Quality control	14.7	14.7	14.7							H
Home sales	29.7	29.7		29.7						I
Export sales	13.3	13.3		13.3						J
General sales	33.9	33.9		33.9						K
Administration expenses	275.6	275.6					75.8	199.8		L
Canteen	29.8	29.8						29.8		M
Research & development	36.4	36.4				36.4				N
Finance charges	51.5	51.5					51.5			O
Management expenses	64.7	64.7	64.7							P
Personnel	22.2	22.2	22.2							Q
Sub-Total	929.5	929.5	101.6	76.9	357.7	36.4	127.3	229.6		
Depreciation	36.3	36.3	3.1	3.8	24.5	2.7	1.1	1.1		R
Total overheads	965.8	965.8	104.7	80.7	382.2	39.1	128.4	230.7		
Profit before tax	578.2	578.2	(60.7)	4019.3	1101.8	(39.1)	(89.0)	(270.1)	(3994.0)	

Figure 2.5   Budget statement - sales director (£000s)

	Total	Sales office	Area A	Area B	Area C	Export
		Mr B	Mr G	Mr H	Mr J	Mr K
Sales						
Manufactured	3950.0	-	1200.0	800.0	1100.0	850.0
Factored	220.0	-	90.0	40.0	60.0	30.0
Total	4170.0	-	1290.0	840.0	1160.0	880.0
Cost of factored goods	70.0	70.0	-	-	-	-
Overhead expenses						
Salaries, etc.	31.2	10.9	4.6	4.6	4.6	6.5
Commission	8.0	2.5	1.5	1.0	1.0	2.0
Pension scheme	3.6	1.5	0.5	0.5	0.5	0.6
Travelling	12.7	4.0	2.0	1.2	2.5	3.0
Entertaining	6.0	2.0	1.0	1.0	1.0	1.0
Rents & rates, etc.	1.6	-	-	0.8	0.8	-
Printing & stationery	1.2	0.4	0.2	0.2	0.2	0.2
Publicity & PR	12.6	12.6	-	-	-	-
	76.9	33.9	9.8	9.3	10.6	13.3
Depreciation	3.8	1.0	0.7	0.7	0.7	0.7
Total expenses	150.7	104.9	10.5	10.0	11.3	14.0
Surplus	4019.3	(104.9)	1279.5	830.0	1148.7	866.0
Number of staff		3	2	2	2	2

Chapter 3
THE FINANCIAL PLANNING TASK

Financial planning, as we saw earlier, covers the broad area of business financing - the needs of a business for various 'types' of money. What these 'types' of money are depends on and is revealed by appropriate analyses of current and planned activities and the direction they will take. The cash flow budget in Figure 3.1 is a basic example of this type of planning, and shows, in its lowest section, the predicted movement of the bank balance and thereby the need for the short-term type of money conventionally provided in the form of bank overdraft, month by month.

Financial planning therefore requires that every aspect of business activity is analysed - revenue and expense items on the one hand and the need for capital on the other. This analysis, however, is not in itself financial planning, though it is often confused with it. Financial planning is the extraction, from the analysis, of the financial consequences of business decisions and activities, and the finding of ways to fulfil the financial needs of the business in the optimum way while ensuring that the enterprise remains profitable. A typical 'source and application of funds' statement is shown in Figure 3.2, which gives a general idea of what is meant, illustrating several ways of obtaining money and several more of spending it. Certain types of financing, such as licensing and HP, are not shown but are nevertheless relevant in appropriate circumstances.

As the whole of a business's activities and future plans have to be analysed for this purpose, the marketing plan has a central role to play. Without it, a great deal of such planning is impossible. Even when a marketing plan is available as a starting point, the financial people have their own set of reasons why their part of the planning is 'impossible'. Financial plans go out of date as quickly as marketing plans and, being more complex, are even harder to revise repeatedly. Some of the problems, on the other hand, may be capable of solution. Part of financial planning relates to the implementation of new projects, as well as the continuation of the business in its present form. In many companies even major new investments can be decided upon with little more than intuitive judgement. Facts and figures are not considered. 'Gut feel' rules. If the top management or owners make decisions in this way, then the most that can be achieved from financial planning is an 'after the event' picture of what will result from the decisions already taken, be it good or bad. Perhaps the ancient custom of beheading the bringer of bad tidings still operates occasionally in the executive suite and discourages too much detailed analysis!

After-the-event analysis is perhaps better than nothing, as many a company has gone out of business because of embarking upon an over-ambitious expansion, a move to a new location, the introduction of a new product or process or even the implementation of inappropriate computer systems. But it is nowhere near as useful as making the planning process part of decision-making in the first place.

A major argument for doing some form of financial planning relates to maintaining good relations with the sources of finance for the business. Banks and financial institutions of all kinds will be approached from time to time by any company in order to raise money for its operations. Banks, although often criticised as conservative and unresponsive, are nevertheless very sensible when it comes to one aspect of how they view their customers. They will often support projects or needs for finance which they know about well in advance, when the same circumstances, revealed at the last minute, will cause them to think twice. For example, if you tell the bank in January that, having done your plans for the year, your £50,000 overdraft facility will need to be raised £10,000/month until it peaks at £100,000 in July, after which it will reduce to £80,000 by December, they will know you have done a great deal of analysis to reach such a conclusion and be ready to believe that you are well in command of events. If, on the other hand, you go to them in May, never having made such a forecast, and ask for £5,000 on the spot to pay the wages at the end of the week, they will begin to wonder whether or not you are really in control! Their reasoning will be that if the company lets that one creep up on it, what else might happen next month? You can see their point, perhaps.

Financial planning, therefore, plays a key role in enabling a company to generate and maintain the confidence of its bankers and investors. Once again, this may initially sound like a big-company activity, without much relevance to smaller businesses. Everyone has bankers, though, and the advice to 'plan ahead' has been found to work well for all sizes of organisation from the personal overdraft up to large corporation financing.

With financial planning as with marketing, the need therefore is strongly coming through for a basis of well-arranged accounting information from which to extract initial figures and, thereafter, monitor performance against the plan. It will be seen to offer the dual benefits of:

(a)   improved management control;
(b)   maintaining the confidence of the organisation's bankers and investors.

Few managers will quibble with the desirability of having sound information. The problem lies in the time-consuming nature of both the initial planning process and the regular revision exercises necessary. In the next chapter we go on to consider in detail the defects of manual planning methods in this context.

The Planning Process

Most companies doing any sort of planning at all stick to a single annual budgeting exercise and thereafter compare results, monthly or quarterly, with the budget figures for sales, expenses, profit and so on. If any aspect of that budget is kept continuously up to date, it tends to be the forecast cash flow, in order to stay one jump ahead of the bank manager.

Figure 3.1   Cash flow budget (£000s)

	Apr	May	Jun	Jul	Aug	Sep	Oct	Nov	Dec	Jan	Feb	Mar	Total
Receipts													
From debtors	20.0	20.0	20.5	20.5	20.5	15.5	20.6	21.6	20.9	22.1	22.7	22.7	247.6
Other income	-	-	0.8	-	-	0.8	-	-	0.8	-	-	0.8	3.2
PAYE deductions	0.8	0.8	0.9	0.9	0.3	0.9	0.9	1.0	1.0	1.0	1.0	1.0	10.5
Realisation of assets	-	-	1.0	-	2.0	-	-	1.0	-	-	-	-	3.0
Loans receivable	-	-	-	-	-	-	-	15.0	-	-	-	-	15.0
Total	20.8	20.8	23.2	21.4	22.8	17.2	21.5	37.6	22.7	23.1	23.7	24.5	279.3
Payments													
Purchases & services	7.6	7.6	8.1	8.6	8.6	6.4	9.1	9.6	9.7	9.7	10.2	10.2	105.4
Wages & salaries	4.9	4.9	5.5	5.5	2.5	5.5	5.5	5.5	6.5	6.5	6.5	6.5	65.8
PAYE paid	-	-	2.5	-	-	2.1	-	-	2.9	-	-	3.0	10.5
VAT paid to C & E	-	2.7	-	-	2.7	17.1	-	2.7	-	-	2.1	-	27.3
Taxation	-	-	-	-	-	-	-	-	-	-	-	3.6	3.6
Dividend	-	-	-	1.8	-	40.0	-	-	-	-	1.0	-	42.8
Capital expenditure	-	5.0	9.0	5.0	10.0	-	-	-	-	-	-	-	29.0
Loan repayments	-	-	1.5	-	-	-	-	-	1.5	-	-	-	3.0
Loan interest	-	-	0.9	-	-	-	-	-	0.9	-	-	-	1.8
Total	12.5	20.2	27.5	20.9	23.8	71.1	14.6	17.8	21.5	16.2	19.8	23.3	289.2
Surplus (deficit)	8.3	0.6	(4.3)	0.5	(1.0)	(53.9)	6.9	19.8	1.2	6.9	3.9	1.2	(9.9)
Balance (overdraft)													
at start	10.9	19.2	19.8	15.5	16.0	15.0	(38.9)	(32.0)	(12.2)	(11.0)	(4.1)	(0.2)	10.9
at end	19.2	19.8	15.5	16.0	15.0	(38.9)	(32.0)	(12.2)	(11.0)	(4.1)	(0.2)	1.0	1.0

Figure 3.2   Source and application of funds statement (£000s)

	1979	1980	1981
Source			
Net profit before taxation	85	150	200
Depreciation	15	40	60
Increase in creditors	10	30	40
Issues of debentures/loans	60	–	100
Increase in bank overdraft	30	30	–
	200	250	400
Application			
Taxation	50	80	100
Capital expenditure	100	100	50
Increase in debtors	20	30	60
Increase in stocks and work in progress	30	20	40
Decrease in bank overdraft	–	–	100
Dividends	–	20	50
	200	250	400

In compiling the budgets, those responsible will have made a whole range of assumptions, covering all the items which have been considered already. Apart from the sales forecasts, which themselves will contain assumptions about price, discounts and volume, it will have been necessary to predict by how much the local authority rates will increase, what will happen to gas, electricity and telephone charges, material and labour costs and many others. Day by day, the predictions will be replaced by fact, and the budget will inevitably become more and more inaccurate.

One way to control this is the idea of so-called 'flexible' budgets. A typical example appears in Figure 3.3, which shows an operating statement in which sales of £2.3m have been achieved against an expectation of £2.5m. As certain expenses, particularly the productive labour and materials content of the items sold, vary directly in proportion with sales, the flexed operating budget takes this into account. Effectively it says: 'If we had budgeted for sales of £2.3m, what would we have budgeted in turn for the other costs and how would we have done against that measure of expectation'. In this particular example the simple reduction in sales is complicated by a price increase with an effect of £100,000 (a). Materials (b) have felt the effects of both reduction in volume and increase in costs. Labour costs (c) have been subject to both increased wages and reduced efficiency. All of this results in (d), £19,000 more gross margin.

In case you are finding this somewhat complicated, take heart. So do most people. But it serves to illustrate the complexity of keeping any type of plan up to date. Assumptions not only change, the changes themselves tend to be interrelated and have consequential effects upon one another. Thus it is normal for companies to leave their budgets alone during the year and simply measure the differences that result from actual operations. Unless there are other planning methods in use alongside the budgets, the horizon to which any predictions have been made gets nearer and nearer as the year progresses. The end of the year is reached with no forward plans at all until, often in a mad scramble, a new year's budget is produced.

Here is probably an appropriate point to enter the 'What's the difference between planning and budgeting?' debate.

In essence, budgets are only more detailed expressions of a portion of a company's plans, normally the first year ahead (or what remains of it). Plans are essentially longer term than budgets and, far from being in the form of figures alone, contain narrative sections about new projects, ideas and methods which are to be implemented over, say three to five years.

Nevertheless, for most companies, the basis of the main plan is planned sales, probably including the introduction of new products and the dropping of old ones as their life cycles progress (see Figures 3.4 and 3.5). After that, production is considered, together with resourcing of raw materials, and items forming part of the sales plan but which are bought in ready-made. This may reveal that more production facilities are needed (e.g. new machines, more factory space) or more warehousing for finished stocks.

Some items in the plan may well not be directly related to sales or production levels. This is particularly true of research and development, which frequently has to be planned even further ahead. Other considerations, apart from sales or production figures, might include the opening of new branches, extending the home market area or building up export trade.

It is also most important that the plan covers capital expenditure as well as the operational aspects of the business. One of the main reasons for planning more than a year ahead is that many projects take much longer than a year to design and implement, and most such projects call for capital expenditure. Obviously the projects and their need for capital must be considered together,

Figure 3.3   Specimen operating statement

	Budget		Actual	
	£000's	%	£000's	%
Sales	2,500	100.0	2,300	100.0
Cost of sales				
Direct materials	1,238	49.5	1,150	30.0
Direct labour				
(productive element)	212	8.5	207	9.0
	1,450	58.0	1,357	59.0
Gross margin	1,050	42.0	943	41.0
Works overheads	75	3.0	92	4.0
Works margin	975	39.0	851	37.0
Other overheads				
Establishment	200	8.0	191	8.3
Administration	213	8.5	207	9.0
Finance	250	10.0	262	11.4
Selling and distribution	137	5.5	122	5.3
Directorate	75	3.0	71	3.1
	875	35.0	853	37.1
Net operating profit (loss)	100	4.0	(2)	(0.1)

Flexed operating budget

	Original budget		Flexed budget		Actual		Variance	
	£000's	%	£000's	%	£000's	%	£000's	%
Sales	2,500	100.0	2,200	100.0	2,300	100.0	100(a)	
Cost of sales								
Direct materials	1,238	49.5	1,089	49.5	1,150	50.0	61(b)	0.5
Direct labour	212	8.5	187	8.5	207	9.0	20(c)	0.5
	1,450	58.0	1,276	58.0	1,357	59.0	81	
Gross margin	1,050	42.0	924	42.0	943	41.0	19(d)	

Figure 3.4   Product and margin mix statement

Product	Sales £000's	Gross margin £000's	Percentages Sales mix	Percentages Margin mix	Difference
Own manufacture					
Cardigans - Retail	260.0	137.8	14.9	18.1	3.2
- Private label	400.0	130.2	22.8	17.1	(5.7)
Pullovers - V-neck	490.0	245.0	28.0	32.1	4.1
- Crew neck	250.0	115.0	14.3	15.1	0.8
Knitted shirts	100.0	62.0	5.7	8.1	2.4
Total own manufacture	1500.0	690.0	85.7	90.5	4.8
Factored					
Pullovers - Heavyweight	190.0	48.5	10.9	6.4	(4.5)
Sports shirts	60.0	24.0	3.4	3.1	(0.3)
Total factored	250.0	72.5	14.3	9.5	(4.8)
Total	£1750.0	£762.5	100.0%	100.0%	-

Figure 3.5   Product life cycle

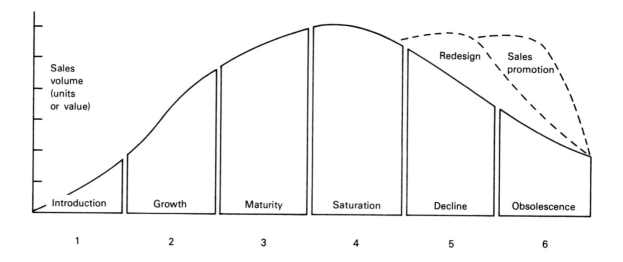

since one affects the other. For example, a decision not to buy some new equipment may require a cut-back in planned sales and production. On the other hand, new equipment may change the amount of labour and materials needed. And the need to plan ahead for any requirements for finance from banks and investors has already been stressed. It must now also be clear that the cash flow budget in Figure 3.1 was indeed a most basic form of financial planning.

In summary, therefore, planning is a much longer term operation than budgeting. It tends to be less detailed because of this, but also has to take into consideration new projects, products and other innovations. It therefore includes many assumptions and ideas which may or may not come to fruition. This makes it inevitable that the plans will have to be changed regularly to keep them in line with reality and with management's latest thinking on the direction the company should take.

Chapter 4
HOW THE COMPUTER CAN HELP

Defects of Manual Planning Methods

Plans have a central role to play in a company's <u>decision-making</u> process. To do this effectively they often need to present a number of alternative evaluations based on different assumptions and different ideas for new projects, product introduction and the like. Here, then, is the fundamental defect of manual planning and budgeting methods, a defect which can often be overcome by the use of computerised methods. The plans, to be of any use, must be easy to produce, over and over again, in a number of 'what if' formats:

'What if we give extra discounts of 5 per cent for orders over £1,000 and this produces increased sales volume of 2 per cent?'
'What happens if it only gives 1 per cent extra?'
'What if we keep the old version going for a further year and hold the price, at the same time deferring its replacement and putting in £100,000 more development on it?'
'What if we open a new warehouse in Birmingham in two years' time which takes 10 per cent of the volume from London and 25 per cent from Manchester, while at the same time sales go up by 15 per cent in each region – how full will the three warehouses be?'
'What does the picture look like if we run all three ideas (above) together next year?'
'What changes if we defer the new warehouse for a further year?'
'What if we put on a second shift with a 30 per cent premium on wages but at the same time stop all production overtime.'

Given a calculator, large sheets of paper, the basic information and peace and quiet, any one of the above questions could be evaluated by most accountants or managers. The work is quite straightforward. It would not be so easy to find the time to work through all of them. To rework them manually as they were being considered and new assumptions or changes emerged would be getting close to impossible. But this is a scenario familiar enough in most companies, and often it results in decisions having to be taken without an adequate evaluation being completed. This is not because there is, as is so often alleged, 'a lack of information on which to base the decision' but rather because there is insufficient time to work through all the options with pen and paper.

Other difficulties with manual systems, which admittedly can be partially alleviated by use of the more sophisticated types of calculator, include working out discounted cash flows and other types of evaluation of returns on investment. A computer, however, will drastically reduce the time taken.

Lastly, once a range of options has been worked out, they need to be looked at from a variety of points of view, normally covering their impact on:

(a) profitability;
(b) cash flow;
(c) capital requirements;
(d) balance sheet.

This in turn brings about a need for a great deal of further work if the full picture is to be collated each time the plans are in any way changed, and further underlines the fact that, with manual methods alone, such an exercise is unlikely to be completed adequately, if at all.

Solutions Offered by Computers

Computers offer a variety of solutions to planning problems. They are often referred to as 'number crunchers', and this is very much the job they do when used in any planning application.

But the use of computers in planning still leaves a number of other problems unchanged. The relevant information for input to the planning activity still has to be available in a suitable form. Chaotic accounting and control systems will not be of much use for providing it. The onus is still on management to think up new projects, ideas and products to bring the plans to life. Assumptions still have to be made about everything from the likely rate of inflation to the possible market for widgets in America.

Without innovative thinking, there can be no plans, computerised or otherwise. Before they can form part of the plans, projects and ideas have to be investigated and costed. There is still a great deal of this and other preliminary work to be done manually. The computer's role is to take over the calculations, and allow a very large number of options to be evaluated in a very short time.

Interfacing accounting and planning software

There is one way in which computers can simplify the information-gathering process itself. This is where computerised accounting systems are being operated in the company where the planning is to be done. But obtaining information from such a source is not as simple as it might appear at first sight.

There are plenty of microcomputer packages (pre-written programs or 'software') available for accounting work, covering such things as sales, bought and nominal (general) ledgers, invoicing, stock control and sales order entry. If the same microcomputer is to be used for both planning and accounting, a special link will normally have to be made between the two types of application (accounting and planning) in order to pass the data from one to the other. This 'interface' will normally be in the form of a program, and the programmer will require detailed knowledge of how the accounting programs are structured in order to know where the required information is held and what form it is in, and to work out how to get at it. As the vendors of package software are usually reluctant to divulge such details, which would make it all too easy for their programs to be pirated, the interface will often need to be programmed by the suppliers of the accounting software. They, in turn, may be unwilling to undertake such work or it may be too expensive. Either way, they will have to become familiar with the planning software as well. Such links, therefore, are not altogether straightforward, although some of the publicity material put out by the microcomputer manufacturer can lead one to believe that the whole area is quite simple. If, however, the accounting software includes some form of 'report generator', this may provide the basis of a solution that is easier to attain in practice. This type of utility program is designed to extract data from files of information in a form specified by the user, and so it may be possible to construct a file of accounting data that can be passed across to the planning system.

Another possible requirement for a link-up arises in circumstances where accounting is carried out in a separate computer. This necessitates some form of information transfer between the computer and the planning microcomputer. The machines themselves may, of course, either be in the same building or in separate locations.

Most microcomputers store data on 5¼" diskettes or 'floppy disks'. This is a storage medium not usually found on larger computers, and so it is unlikely that the required accounting data could be recorded on a diskette in the appropriate format and transferred in this way. It might, of course, be possible to fit the accounting computer with a drive for such a diskette, but again the manufacturer concerned would have to undertake the work and, as a 'one off', it would tend to be expensive. Where the larger 8" diskettes are used, this route may be more flexible. Should the accounting be done on another microcomputer, the problem would be somewhat simplified. Nevertheless, a wholly feasible solution would only result if any of the machines were identical and the accounting system was written in the same programming language and running under the same operating system as the planning system.

Unless there has been a coherent policy on the compatibility of computers in an organisation for some time - which is quite rare - easy data transfer is not likely to be achieved.

Using telecommunications links

A more practical solution often exists through the 'communications' side of the computer. This aspect of the machine is intended to allow connections between installations in various (supposedly) standard forms, and is normally an optional attachment in the form of an additional plug-in printed circuit board that fits inside the computer. The installations may be miles apart, in which case such connections would be carried out over British Telecom telephone lines. To achieve this, devices called 'modems' are needed at each end, different types being required according to the desired speed of transmission of data - dialled or leased telephone lines, two-wire or four-wire connections.

If the computers are close to one another, it may be possible to plug them together with a multi-core cable in the form of one or two coaxial leads (like a TV aerial wire). In the latter case some form of 'local networking' environment may be needed, and this again usually takes the form of a plug-in board in the computers, together with some control software on at least one of the computers in the network.

Any of these direct connections can be envisaged as allowing direct access to data in the other computer, operating with one device emulating a terminal of the other, and extracting data interactively. In simple terms, this would mean that one computer could range over the data in the other, asking questions of it by keyboard action and having the results displayed on its own screen. This is in reality highly complex to achieve, except in a local network between computers of the same model using identical operating systems.

A more practical solution is to aim at a simpler approach in the form of the transfer of files of information. The accounting system might hold a file of budget figures, perhaps giving information monthly on expected sales and costs under a range of coded headings. Alternatively, there might be a file of the last year's actual results under the same headings. The objective of all such transfers is to avoid entering at the keyboard of the planning computer masses of information which already exists elsewhere in computer form.

Another form of information which may be required is that held on data bases by various types of 'information providers'. These give a whole range of economic indicators such as money supply, unemployment levels, price indices and export figures. Many self-contained planning systems on microcomputers can benefit from such statistics, and to obtain them some form of communications link has to be established. The 'host' for a databank, of course, will charge for extraction of the figures, either by a subscription or on a pay-as-you-go basis.

The whole area of communications and data transfer is complex and will normally require either specialist advice and assistance or a reasonable technical understanding of its use, coupled with sufficient time to deal with the problem properly.

Microcomputer Equipment and Programs

Microcomputer equipment itself is generally simple enough to understand, at least for the person capable of an 'O' level maths pass. Part II of this book goes into some detail about how a microcomputer works and how to go about selecting an appropriate model for your needs. Anyone contemplating using a micro for planning should find this quite straightforward if the decision is taken to use standard programs to do the planning work itself. The alternative to this is to write the programs for a planning system oneself, using one of the standard programming languages available with microcomputers. These are normally restricted to BASIC and Pascal, but micro versions of COBOL, the most widely used business language on larger computers, are now becoming available.

Simple though these languages are to learn (BASIC and Pascal that is - COBOL is more difficult), merely mastering the 'vocabulary' and 'syntax' will not make anyone automatically a good programmer. First of all there is a need to precede any programming work with a careful design of the system that is required, expressing the results in some sort of logical form, normally diagrammatical. Such work, rarely undertaken by aspiring amateur programmers, may not be necessary if the computer is only going to be asked to do a few simple calculations, but is absolutely essential if embarking on a complex interlinked system, such as is normally required for planning purposes.

The design work, if done carefully, will normally reveal that the system can be divided into coherent sections, usually called 'modules', which represent individual facets of the work the computer will have to do. In a very simple system, these might only amount to:

(a)   file creation and amendment;
(b)   data entry;

(c)   calculations;

(d)   report production.

Within the modules there might be repetitive areas where the program had to perform the same function again and again at different points in the sequence of operations. One way of achieving this would be to write appropriate program instructions each time the logic required them, but a better method is obviously to write a single routine and 'call' it whenever needed.

These simple examples of design and structure in programming are intended to illustrate the care that is needed if a user intends to program himself. If it suggests to the reader that this may not be the best course of action, all the better. Most amateur programming takes the form of classic 'wheel re-invention', all too often resulting in a new version which is square rather than round!

Standard programs should always be considered first, whatever the application that is to be run on the computer. In choosing a computer, therefore, it is essential to be aware of what standard programs are available to run on it. Many people consequently believe that it is correct to select the software first and then buy the computer it runs on, and this is usually the most sensible course of action.

When choosing software, you will usually be given a demonstration of its function. However satisfactory that may be, there is something else to look for, and that is the documentation. Any standard software will come with some sort of manual which sets out to describe what it does and how to use it. The programs may all look simple enough in the showroom, when demonstrated by an expert, but when you get back to the office there will be a need for a simple step-by-step guide on how to use them. This obviously also applies to the microcomputer itself.

Some manuals are clearly and logically written, well organised and easy to understand. Most are not. Look carefully at the documentation before buying. Vendors of microcomputer systems cannot afford to provide the level of training and support that is supplied by sellers of larger systems. There may be someone to telephone if there is a problem, but you will be unlikely to get much in the way of direct tuition on a system which costs, say £3,000, and you certainly will not get free follow-up or repeat visits to check how you are progressing and help with problems.

Microcomputers in Planning

After all these cautionary warnings, how can the computer help with planning? Its real strength lies in its ability to cope with many versions of the same plan. Calculations done with one set of assumptions or data can be quickly rerun with another. Different calculations can be included, either in substitution for the original ones or as a second set alongside, and the plans re-evaluated.

Such a capability is not only useful for trying out a variety of options when constructing a plan in the first place, but can also be employed to update the plan regularly as circumstances change, actual results become available and individual decisions are modified. In this way, plans can be kept in line with reality and the latest thinking, in such a way that the outcome of the planned operation of the company is always known. To achieve this, most planning systems operate as some form of computer-based matrix, which can be thought of as a large sheet of paper divided into rows and columns.

Planning systems may also have other features which allow consolidations to be carried out. These might be necessary where a divisional structure is in force

(Figure 4.1), or where a holding company has a number of subsidiaries (Figure 4.2) for which individual plans are drawn up. Each plan can be maintained separately and the results regularly consolidated to provide a general picture.

In the final analysis the idea behind using computers to help with planning is to reduce the time it takes to generate the figures and thereby to make more time available for their study, analysis and revision. From all this, better decision-making should result.

Figure 4.1   Planning for divisional structure

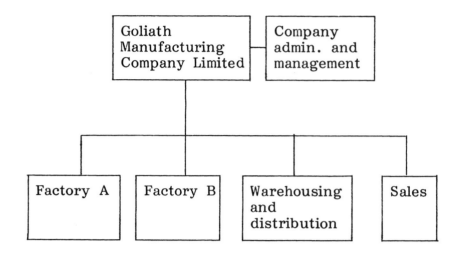

Figure 4.2   Planning for holding company with
subsidiaries

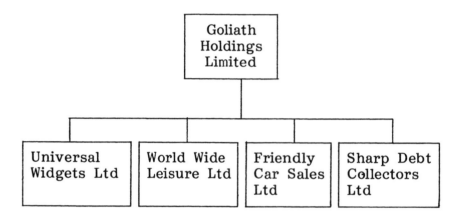

Chapter 5
STANDARD PLANNING SOFTWARE

Most of the available software in this area falls under the general heading of 'financial modelling'. This is not a wholly accurate description of its function, as it covers both the areas of marketing and financial planning as defined earlier in the book. Strictly speaking, it could more appropriately be referred to as 'corporate modelling'. However the term 'financial modelling' is in general use and from now on, therefore, we shall use it, as it will bring to mind appropriate software when talking to suppliers.

Financial modelling on computers has been around a long time. Packages were available in the early sixties on large mainframe computers. Such computer systems then cost well into six figures, and, with what we can now see was cheap labour, the relative expense of programming was much less conspicuous. The systems operated in 'batch' mode, as did most computers in those days. Data was fed in on punched cards, the program did all the calculations and reports were produced. If anything went wrong in the middle, the whole process often came to a halt and, after the fault in the computer or the program had been isolated and fixed, everything had to be rerun. Operating in this way, the user of the financial model and the information it produced was very much at arm's length from the computer, with large numbers of experts making things happen (or fail to happen) for him.

Today's Solution

Everything is now very different. It is no secret that equipment costs have fallen drastically over the last few years because of the widespread use of micro-electronics and the availability of cheap micro-circuits. What used to fill a large air-conditioned computer room can now sit on a desk. No army of experts is required. In line with these equipment changes, software has changed markedly as well. There are now plenty of financial modelling packages on the market and, as an example, one of them, MasterModeller, will be discussed later in this chapter. The packages range in price from around £50 to £1,000 and run on microcomputer systems of the desk-top variety costing approximately £1,000 to £2,000. A typical high performance desk-top system, including planning software, can therefore cost up to £4,000, although this can be more depending on the actual equipment specified.

The software itself is no longer written to operate in 'batch' mode, but allows the user to interact directly with it, with actions at the keyboard resulting immediately in displays on the screen. These actions range from the entry of command statements to get the programs to run, through the input of statements which comprise the calculating logic of the financial model, to simple submission of the data on which the calculations will be based.

This brief description gives the first indication of what elements of equipment are required to run financial modelling software. Already mentioned are:

(a)   the computer itself, which is the 'black box' in which all the calculations are done and via which all the other equipment and actions are controlled;

(b)   a keyboard, normally in typewriter format, through which to enter data, commands and program statements;

(c)   a screen on which to view what is entered at the keyboard, where prompts from the computer on what to do next are displayed, as are results of some calculations.

In addition, some form of long-term storage for programs and data is needed, and this normally comes in the form of $5\frac{1}{4}$" diskettes and diskette 'drives' (in which they run). The drives hold the diskette on a spindle and rotate it over a reading and recording 'head'. The diskette is simply inserted through a slot. Most microcomputers use such diskettes, on which characters are magnetically recorded and read by the computer. Programs are provided therefore in the form of pre-recorded diskettes.

Lastly, there needs to be a printer to produce reports, program listings and any other output that requires to be read and studied at leisure. Various options are available for each of these devices. The computer itself can have different amounts of memory - the area in which data and programs are stored while operations proceed. Standard software will have a minimum memory requirement in order to operate and this will (usually) be clearly stated by the supplier. In essence, the programs and the data take up a certain amount of space in memory and will not work unless it is available.

The keyboard is often part of the computer itself and is not bought as a separate item. Different keyboards have different numbers of keys for certain special functions over and above the standard 'QWERTY' layout. The most common extra is a calculator format numeric keypad for fast data entry.

Screens can be anything from an old black and white TV to a specialist colour monitor. To drive a domestic TV display, most microcomputers need an extra circuit board to make the connection.

The main decision to be made about diskette drives is on the number to have. Most microcomputers have two drives. The software supplier will usually advise how many drives are needed for his programs, both as a minimum and for ideal operations. A sensible minimum is always two drives to allow single diskette copies to be made for security purposes. The more drives you have the less you will need to replace one disk with another during operation and the more smoothly everything will proceed. In addition, if one breaks down, you may still be able to continue to operate on the other(s).

Printers rise in cost roughly in proportion to the speed and quality of output required. A typewriter-quality word-processing printer might cost £1,500 to £3,000, whereas a simple 80 character wide dot-matrix printer could be around £200 to £300. Another point to consider is not simply speed and quality but the amount of printing needed. The cheap and simple printers are sometimes not 'continuously rated' and are therefore not constructed of sufficient quality to print non-stop all day.

The choice of equipment on which to run the chosen software is therefore related both to the needs of the software itself and to the way in which you intend to use it. The fundamental point, and the reason why some description of hardware appears in the software chapter, is that the hardware must be chosen to fit the software, not the other way around.

How the Software Works

How does the software work? We have already described it as some kind of large computerised sheet of paper in a matrix format, containing some number of rows and columns.

The available types of computer program for use in financial modelling break down into two main categories. These are:

(a) 'electronic spreadsheet' modellers;
(b) logical modellers.

Certain systems also offer additional facilities, sometimes as extra cost options. These cover such things as presentation graphics and various forms of aids to decision-making, such as facilities for sensitivity analysis on figures produced from the models.

The best known spreadsheet modellers are Lotus 123 and Supercalc. The term 'spreadsheet' refers to the mode of operation of this type of model. The screen of the computer acts as a window on to a large sheet on which the data are recorded and calculations are made, thereby drawing on the similarity between this and an accountant working on a huge sheet of analysis paper. The dimensions of the electronic sheet are in the form of a matrix of 127 columns and 9999 rows. Each element of this matrix is called a cell. Each cell can be used to contain directly entered data or a formula which calculates a result. Changing any data or formula causes all affected areas of the model to be recalculated automatically.

Logical modellers operate in a more formal and structured manner, and require more understanding of computer use than do spreadsheets. Logical modellers are normally constructed from a number of separate 'files'. The most crucial of these are the logic file and the data file. The logic file defines the way all the calculations will be done for the rows and columns of the model. Generally, therefore, there is no predefined structure to the matrix, other than a maximum number of cells. Any combination of columns and rows that falls within this can be used.

A logical modeller is normally provided with a special simplified programming language with which to write all the logic statements. This is usually very little different from the English language and mathematical statements that you would naturally use to write equivalent statements on paper. It has to be learnt, but is not very difficult.

The more detailed example of the use of MasterModeller below will furnish a fuller explanation. In summary the essential differences between logical modellers and spreadsheets are:

	Spreadsheets	Logical Modelling Programs
Advantages	Relatively inexpensive	Better for multiple data sets and reports
	Easy to learn	
	Cursor cell reference	Offer more complex financial functions
	Entire worksheet viewable	Handle file consolidation and report formatting better
	Good range of mathematical functions and (increasingly) financial functions	Greater capacity and speed of calculation
Disadvantages	Logic, data and reports all on the same worksheet with consequent difficulty in producing complex reports	Difficult to learn, often requiring programming knowledge
	Less flexible in handling 'variables' which must be identified by their location in the worksheet	Few non-financial functions
		Necessity to compile logic
	Limited branching and iteration possibilities	
Main Use	Medium size models	Good for large models, particularly with multiple data files requiring consolidation

MasterModeller

MasterModeller is one of a number of logical modellers on the market and is chosen here as an example with which the authors are most familiar through using it in their management consultancy work. Whether or not it is the most suitable for the reader's particular circumstances is something that must be determined separately. Part II of this book will be helpful in reaching such a decision.

Below is a schematic overview of the various components in MasterModeller. The system can either be controlled by the user in the individual modules or the central job language can be used to control the operation automatically.

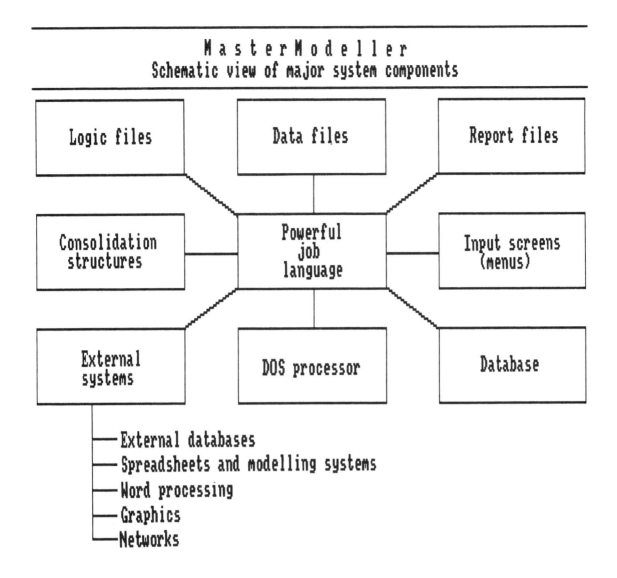

MasterModeller
Schematic view of major system components

Examination of the above view will indicate the essential differences between modelling systems and spreadsheet systems. For repetitive use, particularly by inexperienced modellers, models written in modelling languages are much easier than spreadsheet based models for the user.

One simple use of MasterModeller might be that shown in Figure 5.1. Note the three columns and numerous rows. From Figure 5.1, an immediate question arises on how to deal with sales. They could be put in financial terms. Alternatively, sales units and unit value could be included separately for each product. The latter method makes re-running the model at different volumes and prices an easy matter. All that has to be done is to submit revised values and recalculate. If sales values in total had been used, a lot of calculations would need to be done externally (possibly using the calculator and paper we were trying to dispense with) before submitting data to the computer. Rule one, 'Let the computer do the work', is obvious enough.

Figure 5.1 Simple use of MasterModeller

	1984	1985	1986

Sales
Product A
Product B
Product C
Total sales

   Less: selling expenses

Sub-total

   Less: distribution expenses

Sub-total

   Less: cost of goods sold

GROSS PROFIT

Expenses
Rent and rates
Heat, light and power
Salaries
Wages
Telephone and postage
General
Total expenses

NET PROFIT

The MasterModeller logic behind Figure 5.1 appears in the printout shown in Figure 5.2.   Lines starting with a "." are comments which have a descriptive function only and in no way affect the operation of the programs.   In the example, the separation between unit price and sales volume has been made to allow easy input of data for different assumptions.

Figure 5.2   Printout of Figure 5.1

```
TITLE "Goliath Sales & Manufacturing Co. Ltd."
PERIODS 3, YEARS(1984,1986)
  .                                 INPUT DATA
  .                                 **********
  .                                 SALES
  .                                 *****
L1     'Sales Volume:A'
L2     'Sales Volume:B'
L3     'Sales Volume:C'

L4     'Unit Price:A'
L5     'Unit Price:B'
L6     'Unit Price:C'
  .                                 EXPENSES
  .                                 ********
L7     'Rent & Rates'
L8     'Electricity'
L9     'Salaries'
L10    'Wages'
L11    'Telephone & Postage'
L12    'General'
L13    'Distribution'
  .                                 CALCULATIONS
  .                                 ************
  .                                 SALES
  .                                 *****
L14    'Sales Value:A' = L1 * L4
L15    'Sales Value:B' = L2 * L5
L16    'Sales Value:C' = L3 * L6
L17    'Total Sales Value' = SUM(L14,L16)
  .                                 COSTS & EXPENSES
  .                                 ****************
L18    'Selling Expenses' = L17*3/100
L19    'Sub Total1' = L17-L18
L20    'Sub Total2' = L19-L13
L21    'Cost of Sales' = L14*25/100 + L15*15/100 + L16*30/100
L22    'Total Expenses' = SUM(L8,L12)
  .                                 GROSS PROFIT
  .                                 ***********
L23    'Gross Profit' = L20-L21
  .                                 NET PROFIT
  .                                 **********
L24    'Net Profit' = L23-L22
  .                                 FINANCIAL RATIOS
  .                                 ****************
L25    'Expenses as % Sales' = L22*100/L17
L26    'Gross Profit as % Sales' = L23*100/L17
L27    'Net Profit as % Sales' = L24*100/L17
```

This series of statements is called the 'logic file' and specifies all the items for which data will be entered. Some items, however, will be seen to have a "=" sign after their description, the first of these being row L14. This indicates that the value of the item will be calculated by the computer, in this case by multiplying (signified by the * symbol) row L1 by row L4. Row L17 is another calculated value, with the SUM (L14,L16) indicating that rows L14 through L16 (i.e. L14, L15 and L16) are to be added together.

Row L18 is arrived at by multiplying row L17 by 3 and dividing by 100, thereby giving 3 per cent of row L17. In the logic as it stands in Figure 5.2 the rule of letting the computer do the work has been broken each time percentage calculations are needed. The percentage calculation is embedded in the logic, requiring it to be amended for different values to be tried.

Figure 5.3 shows this defect corrected, and it also shows that to do it has not necessitated the renumbering of any rows below the changed item (new row L13a). It is easy to see that similar changes need to be made to L21, to allow the separate input of individual gross profit percentages. This has been done in Figure 5.4 and again no row re-numbering has been necessary.

The trouble is that the idea of using microcomputers is often a very attractive one and it is hard to resist the temptation to get started. Just as we have been adding rows, we had better amend the rules as well. The rules now become:

1. Know what you want before you start.
2. Let the computer do the work.

The manual for MasterModeller is of course provided in addition to the manuals which come with the microcomputer itself. They describe how to operate it and how to use the MSDOS or PCDOS environment, the general support area for the computer and the modelling system.

These manuals, though comprehensive, require a higher degree of technical understanding than is needed for effective use of MasterModeller. There is no need for the user to learn how to program the computer, but knowledge of how to use the filing system is helpful, and facility with the processes for formatting and copying diskettes is essential.

The filing system controls the disposition of data on the diskettes. It allows old files of data to be removed, thus freeing space on the diskettes for other use. It provides a means of displaying lists of files on diskettes such that the user can keep control of what is being stored. Some of these functions are duplicated within MasterModeller but additional reading of the manuals may be needed to master this area. One feature of particular use, setting the date (which subsequently is written on all files created), is done automatically by MasterModeller.

Again, the more experienced computer user will be well familiar with the sort of procedures that are commonly used with larger machines to copy data and print files and programs as precautions against their loss or destruction. While it is often felt that these routines are not relevant to microcomputers, they are, in fact, much more important, as the micro has many fewer built-in fail-safe procedures than larger computers. This makes the loss or corruption of data or programs, which may have taken many hours of laborious work at the keyboard to enter in the first place, much more likely. There is less protection against mistaken erasure of files. Fewer questions are asked of the user by the computer and there are fewer escape routes if wrong instructions are given. Hardware failures are more likely to result in loss or corruption of data and so on. When he was still quite new to such packages, one of the authors accidentally deleted three files of information, all of which had luckily been

Figure 5.3   Correction of Figure 5.2

```
TITLE "Goliath Sales & Manufacturing Co. Ltd."
PERIODS 3, YEARS(1984,1986)
.                               INPUT DATA
.                               **********
.                               SALES
.                               *****
L1    'Sales Volume:A'
L2    'Sales Volume:B'
L3    'Sales Volume:C'

L4    'Unit Price:A'
L5    'Unit Price:B'
L6    'Unit Price:C'
.                               EXPENSES
.                               ********
L7    'Rent & Rates'
L8    'Electricity'
L9    'Salaries'
L10   'Wages'
L11   'Telephone & Postage'
L12   'General'
L13   'Distribution'
L13a  'Selling Exps % Sales'
.                               CALCULATIONS
.                               ************
.                               SALES
.                               *****
L14   'Sales Value:A' = L1 * L4
L15   'Sales Value:B' = L2 * L5
L16   'Sales Value:C' = L3 * L6
L17   'Total Sales Value' = SUM(L14,L16)
.                               COSTS & EXPENSES
.                               ***************
L18   'Selling Expenses' = L17*L13a/100
L19   'Sub Total1' = L17-L18
L20   'Sub Total2' = L19-L13
L21   'Cost of Sales' = L14*25/100 + L15*15/100 + L16*30/100
L22   'Total Expenses' = SUM(L8,L12)
.                               GROSS PROFIT
.                               ***********
L23   'Gross Profit' = L20-L21
.                               NET PROFIT
.                               **********
L24   'Net Profit' = L23-L22
.                               FINANCIAL RATIOS
.                               ***************
L25   'Expenses as % Sales' = L22*100/L17
L26   'Gross Profit as % Sales' = L23*100/L17
L27   'Net Profit as % Sales' = L24*100/L17
```

Figure 5.4   Amended Figure 5.3

```
TITLE "Goliath Sales & Manufacturing Co. Ltd."
PERIODS 3, YEARS(1984,1986)
  .                              INPUT DATA
  .                              **********
  .                              SALES
  .                              *****
L1    'Sales Volume:A'
L2    'Sales Volume:B'
L3    'Sales Volume:C'

L4    'Unit Price:A'
L5    'Unit Price:B'
L6    'Unit Price:C'
L6a   'Sales cost % UP:A'
L6b   'Sales cost % UP:B'
L6c   'Sales cost % UP:C'
  .                              EXPENSES
  .                              ********
L7    'Rent & Rates'
L8    'Electricity'
L9    'Salaries'
L10   'Wages'
L11   'Telephone & Postage'
L12   'General'
L13   'Distribution'
L13a  'Selling Exps % Sales'
  .                              CALCULATIONS
  .                              ************
  .                              SALES
  .                              *****
L14   'Sales Value:A' = L1 * L4
L15   'Sales Value:B' = L2 * L5
L16   'Sales Value:C' = L3 * L6
L17   'Total Sales Value' = SUM(L14,L16)
  .                              COSTS & EXPENSES
  .                              ****************
L18   'Selling Expenses' = L17*L13a/100
L19   'Sub Total1' = L17-L18
L20   'Sub Total2' = L19-L13
L21   'Cost of Sales' = L14*L6a/100 + L15*L6b/100 + L16*L6c/100
L22   'Total Expenses' = SUM(L8,L12)
  .                              GROSS PROFIT
  .                              ************
L23   'Gross Profit' = L20-L21
  .                              NET PROFIT
  .                              **********
L24   'Net Profit' = L23-L22
  .                              FINANCIAL RATIOS
  .                              ****************
L25   'Expenses as % Sales' = L22*100/L17
L26   'Gross Profit as % Sales' = L23*100/L17
L27   'Net Profit as % Sales' = L24*100/L17
```

printed out beforehand. All that was then needed was the extra work of re-keying them, rather than the alternative of deriving them again from scratch.

Further amendment to the rules is needed in the light of all this. We now have:

1. Know what you want before you start.
2. Plan ahead carefully, make notes before you do anything and print immediately afterwards.
3. Copy diskettes regularly.
4. Let the computer do the work.

Returning to the example financial model, we left it as shown in Figure 5.3. How did the rows of logic get into the computer? They were entered in via the keyboard, using an aid called the 'editor', which operates like a word-processor, giving facilities to add, amend and delete lines of text and numbers. This aid is employed for all aspects of MasterModeller file creation and amendment, such activity covering logic, data, report, job and consolidation specifications, and other features which will be discussed later.

Once entered, the logic has to be 'compiled' to translate it into a useable form for the computer. All this means is that the logic statements in their 'English' format are converted into another set of statements in a form the computer can work with directly. In this form they are not available to the user on the screen, but this is not important.

To compile the logic, the user simply hits one of the function keys on the keyboard and the rest is automatic. A highlighted bar appears on the screen as MasterModeller progresses through the logic, to show which line is being compiled. Checks are made on the logic and any errors present are revealed.

In order to use the logic thereafter, the user needs to key in some data for it to work on. In order to make this easier, MasterModeller provides a VIEW mode which is obtained by use of the function keys. Figure 5.5a shows the view screen with the data already entered.

All that has to be done now to complete the calculations in the model is to give the CALC command. The results of this will no doubt be needed in the form of a printed report and to do this a report specification may be produced. We will look at this shortly, but it is normally best to use the VIEW mode until the model has been checked thoroughly. VIEW mode is a powerful facility as it allows the user to enter temporary data and view the effect of the calculations on screen. Alternatively, the command LIST will cause a printed report to be produced in a crude format which is adequate for checking the results but not usually good enough for final presentation.

If the logic or data is deficient in any way, it will be revealed at this stage by the appearance of unexpected or distorted values or error messages. This enables appropriate corrections to be made and the model re-run to check that the problems have been eradicated.

Although the model covers a period of three years, and therefore needs three entries of data for each row, various forms of shorthand may be used. Row L1, for example, may be entered as L1=GROW (3000,10) and this instructs MasterModeller to increase the amount for each cell in the row by 10 per cent (compound) starting from 3000. Row L2 was entered as L2 = 9000, meaning that each cell in the row has the same value of 9000. Other figures are entered directly on to the view screen. Although useful during development, VIEW mode is not suitable for use in the final model. Therefore an alternative method for use in fully developed models is provided in the form of input menu screens as seen in Figure 5.5b.

Figure 5.5a View screen with data entered

Goliath Sales & Manufacturing Co. Ltd. C1

Command:

	1984	1985	1986
L1 Sales Volume:A	3000.00	3300.00	3630.00
L2 Sales Volume:B	9000.00	9000.00	9000.00
L3 Sales Volume:C	5000.00	5500.00	6050.00
L4 Unit Price:A	20.00	20.00	20.00
L5 Unit Price:B	8.00	7.00	6.00
L6 Unit Price:C	45.00	50.00	60.00
L6A Sales cost % UP:A	30.00	30.00	30.00
L6B Sales cost % UP:B	20.00	20.00	20.00
L6C Sales cost % UP:C	27.00	27.00	27.00
L7 Rent & Rates	38750.00	42500.00	59000.00
L8 Electricity	21000.00	25200.00	30240.00
L9 Salaries	76400.00	86040.00	96644.00
L10 Wages	85300.00	95830.00	107413.00
L11 Telephone & Postage	18500.00	22200.00	26640.00
L12 General	3000.00	3300.00	3630.00
L13 Distribution	22000.00	25300.00	29095.00
L13A Selling Exps % Sale	4.00	4.00	5.00
L14 Sales Value:A	60000.00	66000.00	72600.00
L15 Sales Value:B	72000.00	63000.00	54000.00
L16 Sales Value:C	225000.00	275000.00	363000.00

1 CALC 2 EXIT 3 TOP 4 EDIT 5 BOTTOM 6 ALIAS 7 HELP

Figure 5.5b   Input menu screen

INPUT MENU

SALES DATA:	1984	1985	1986
Sales Volume:A	3000	3300	3630
Sales Volume:B	9000	9000	9000
Sales Volume:C	5000	5500	6050
Unit Price:A	20	20	20
Unit Price:B	8	7	6
Unit Price:C	45	50	60
EXPENSES:			
Rent & Rates	38750	42500	59000
Electricity	21000	25200	30240
Salaries	76400	86040	96644
Wages	85300	95830	107413
Telephone & Postage	18500	22200	26640
General	3000	3300	3630
COST:			
Distribution	22000	25300	29095
Selling Exps % Sales	60000	66000	72600

OK? Y/N ▮

Once the logic is complete, a report can be produced. It is a good idea for the user to start the design of his model by <u>first</u> sketching out the report format that will be required at the end. This is recommended because the best guide to the operation and contents of the model is what kind of output is required at the end of all the work.

The creation of high quality reports is made easy as the system automatically provides a report based on the logic of the model being developed. This may then be polished up using the editor. Figure 5.6 shows a report produced for our example.

The work of controlling the reading and saving of data files, the input of data and the printing of reports is done by a 'job'. This is written (again using the editor) in a simple command language. Consolidation of data is also a simple matter thanks to the sophisticated facilities available.

Once this point has been reached different data files can be created by copying and altering files or by entering completely new sets of data. Similarly, the logic can be modified and stored in separate logic files for alternative calculation methods. Results can also be displayed in graphical form instead of being printed. Many more advanced financial calculations are available, but they are best understood by actual use of the system.

As experience builds up, more complex calculations and models can be attempted. The company that produces MasterModeller regularly receives from users details of new applications of the system which they have not tried or thought of themselves. There is already said to be one company using the system for the consolidation of figures from 200 subsidiary companies.

Figure 5.6   Report specification file

```
DATE:              Goliath Sales & Manufacturing Co. Ltd.            Page 1


                              1984            1985            1986

SALES & COSTS
=============

Sales Value:A               60,000          66,000          72,600
Sales Value:B               72,000          63,000          54,000
Sales Value:C              225,000         275,000         363,000
                           -------         -------         -------

Total Sales Value          357,000         404,000         489,600

less
Selling Expenses            14,280          16,160          24,480
                           -------         -------         -------

Sub Total1                 342,720         387,840         465,120

less
Distribution                22,000          25,300          29,095
                           -------         -------         -------

Sub Total2                 320,720         362,540         436,025

less
Cost of Sales               93,150         106,650         130,590

                           -------         -------         -------

Gross Profit               227,570         255,890         305,435

less
Total Expenses             204,200         232,570         264,567
                           =======         ======          =======

Net Profit                  23,370          23,320          40,868
                           =======         ======          =======

FINANCIAL RATIOS
================

Expenses as % Sales          57.2            57.6            54.0
Gross Profit as % Sales      63.7            63.3            62.4
Net Profit as % Sales         6.5             5.8             8.3
```

43

Strategy Modelling

The main use of modelling has been to reduce administration workload in calculations involved in budgetary control systems. The reason for systems-based modelling being such a major application area for models is that logic is defined, data exists and there is usually a need to repeat calculations regularly and often a need to consolidate results together from varying sources.

However, the most likely future development of modelling applications will be in the strategic decision taking area. Financial performance in a business is more likely to be influenced by better decisions based on information used at the time of the decision taken.

An example of this approach is Strategy Modeller, which helps decision taking at director or senior executive level.

This is a structured model which works as a stand-alone model but is written using the capabilities of MasterModeller or its run time derivative. It uses many of the features of MasterModeller outlined in the schematic diagram:

- data input through menu screens;
- logic files separate and controlled automatically by job files;
- screens used to view and revise plan data.

Reports have several options to allow flexibility. Plan data files, created from base data files, can be converted into base data files for year on year planning.

The model effectively consists of a great deal of preformed logic which uses data input of profit and loss account in added value format and balance sheet. From this data input the model creates a source and applications of funds statement and a set of interlinked financial and productivity ratios.

A strategy flow diagram, shown opposite, outlines how the system works.

STRATEGY FLOW DIAGRAM

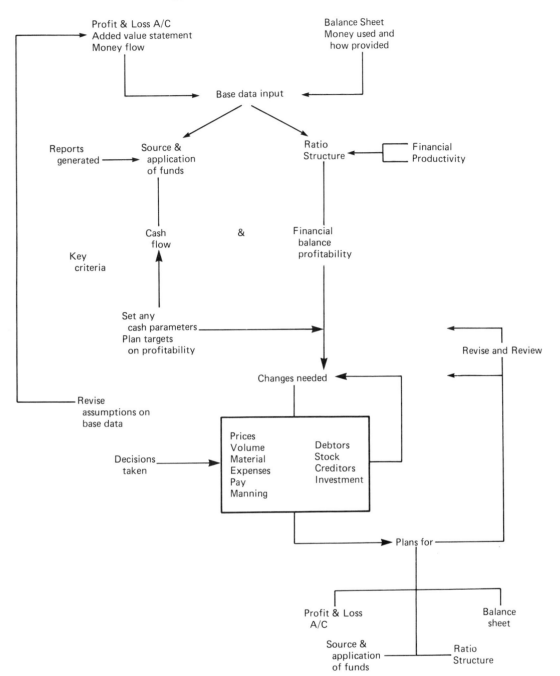

From this base data Strategy Modeller allows a goal setting approach to improving business performance. All model systems allow 'what if' changes to be made and results calculated - Strategy Modeller does this. However, its unique feature is that it allows a profit target to be set, for which one of five profitability ratios can be used as well as £ profit.

Target Profit

This base is often important, particularly where a company is growing or needs to improve its current position by specific sums of money.
Beginning with PL ......

```
┌──────────────────────────────────────────────────────────────────┐
│  ┌────────────────────────────────────────────────┐   Plan:       │
│  │ CHOOSE THE MAJOR CRITERIA FOR YOUR NEW PLAN     │   PLDEMOS     │
│  │ ───────────────────────────────────────────     │               │
│  │  YOUR NEW PLAN CAN HAVE JUST ONE OF THESE 6 CRITERIA │ Base:     │
│  │ ─────────────────────────────────────────────── │   BADEMOS    │
│  │                              Base Year Value     │               │
│  │  1. Profit % Capital.................. 18.91     │               │
│  │                                                  │               │
│  │  2. Profit % Assets................... 11.72     │               │
│  │                                                  │               │
│  │  3. Profit % Sales.................... 8.80      │               │
│  │                                                  │               │
│  │  4. Operating Profit % Assets......... 12.26     │               │
│  │                                                  │               │
│  │  5. Shareholders % Return............. 15.65     │               │
│  │                                                  │               │
│  │  6. Actual Profit Target.............. 66        │               │
│  │   (Key "0" to EXIT)    WHICH CRITERIA? (1,2,3,4,5,6) 6 │          │
│  │                                                  │               │
│  │                       VALUE FOR PLAN YEAR?  91.00 │              │
│  │                                                  │               │
│  │              (C)ontinue  ▮                        │               │
│  └────────────────────────────────────────────────┘               │
└──────────────────────────────────────────────────────────────────┘
```

Enter the Criteria numbers (1.....6) followed by the rate for the Plan.

Hit 'C' to continue.

After selecting this target the model allows a series of assumptions to be made on items such as other income, capital spending, loan repayments or increases, tax rates and dividend % of profit, depreciation and interest rates. Cash and overdraft limits can also be changed.

After these assumption changes the model calculates the list of decision options related to decisions to:

- get money in   - volume
                   - prices

- control costs   - cost changes on three spending headings and three expense headings

- control pay   - headcount and pay rates under two headings

- manage cash   - debtor, creditor, stock control and investment under three headings.

Once the assumptions and rates have been fed into the system, the model will calculate the decisions needed to achieve the objectives set for profit or profitability within the assumptions made. The screen below will appear:

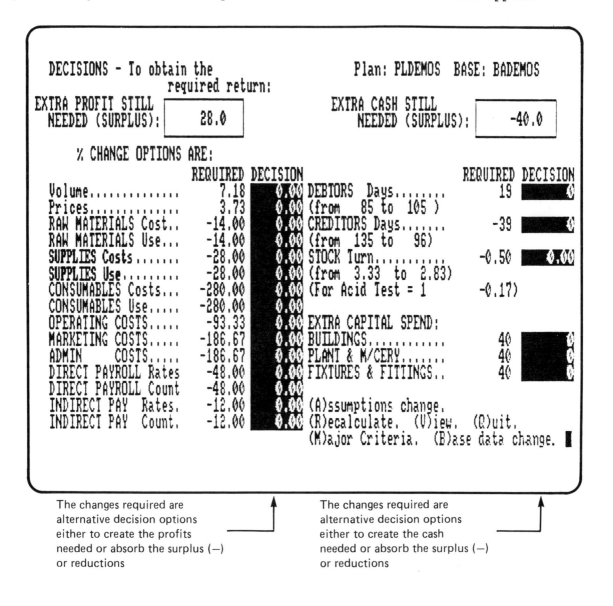

The changes required are alternative decision options either to create the profits needed or absorb the surplus (−) or reductions

The changes required are alternative decision options either to create the cash needed or absorb the surplus (−) or reductions

To operate the strategy planning system, various decision options or mixes of decision options can be used.

These decision options are fed into the decision columns of this screen:

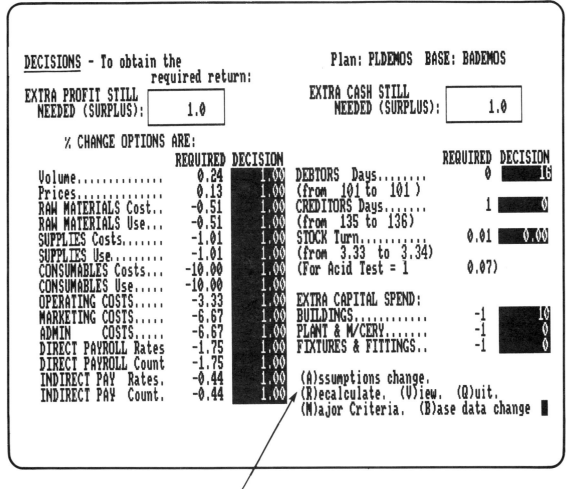

These are figures for PLDEMOS.

The system will recalculate the strategy plan each time there is a change. It is usually better to solve the profit equation first before dealing with balance sheet decisions.

Options remaining to achieve a target after taking decisions are shown for an individual plan. Where several plans are printed a table of options remaining is printed.

Selecting (V) = view allows the profit and loss account, balance sheet, source and application of funds plus ratios to be viewed. Other options – changes can be reviewed and made by selecting the appropriate key. Any single decision or combination of decisions can be made and the model will recalculate the results and options required to achieve the target.

Cost increases can be fed in and all options to achieve the target are recalculated. At any time the effect of the decisions can be viewed on the screen. Models can be saved at any time and up to five can be printed out side by side.

The Strategy Modeller system uses menu screens for ease of operation. Option menus cover data input and changing, target setting, printing consolidation, interfacing to graphics and file maintenance.

A variation on Strategy Modeller is Strategy Analyser which analyses the decisions involved in a two year profit/loss account period and uses the three related balance sheets. This shows the key decision factors on prices - volume costs, expenses, headcount and pay rates - which have affected decisions. The key ratios are calculated and changes presented.

This type of goal seeking modelling has been used in a Market Strategy model to cope with up to 400 products in 20 groups. This model uses added value as the target - calculated in Strategy Modeller. This model works on product-by-product bases showing what changes in volume, price, costs and overhead recovery are needed to achieve a target added value. Constant recalculation as product decisions are made is a feature of this model.

To get the importance of this decision support modelling approach into perspective it is likely that profits will be affected by at least 20%, usually 50% and often as high as 80% as a result of 1% beneficial changes in seven key decision factors. This highlights the financial justification for developing management decision support models.

Modelling Developments/Applications

The importance of modelling to improve the quality of decision taking will continue to develop for several reasons:

- Hardware, which is becoming cheaper, will have larger RAM and be able to process more data faster and hard disks will allow larger quantities of data to be handled more easily.

- Software - spreadsheets for modelling has developed as a popular use for microcomputers. This is leading companies and individuals to look for more sophisticated systems now they have learned of the benefits of modelling.

- Software modelling systems, although needing more learning time, now use menus, have self-contained data bases, link to graphic packages, work with word processing software and link to networked systems. Probably of more significance is the way modelling systems can be used as a form of programming language and as knowledge communications systems. This allows more sophisticated models to be developed which contain reasoning capability and rules of application.

- Models have been used to improve commercial awareness and for financial learning programmes. This has improved the understanding of the logic of the business and decision process - this creates wider use of models.

Modelling systems will play a significant role in bringing to an end the days of chauffeur driven computing. As managers grow more confident in understanding the logic of decisions, the availability of data and the value of information to improve performance, then more applications of modelling will develop. As this process develops, it will be important to understand that the cost of the time involved will outweigh the hardware and software costs. Against this background the design of models will require more planning and attention to detail.

Chapter 6
PLANNING A NEW BUSINESS

This chapter is slanted towards those actually considering starting a business. But it can equally be used for planning and assessing a diversification project for an existing business or simply as a first practical exercise in operating a financial planning system on a microcomputer.

The availability of financial modelling packages for micros now makes possible the application of computer methods to all sizes of businesses right from the beginning. Indeed, it is when contemplating a new business venture that almost every aspect of the proposed operation of the new company is open to question, and here the ability, by means of a modelling package, to see the results of many different approaches to getting the business started gives the user a great advantage.

The fostering of new businesses from start-up through the initial difficult trading years is currently a topic in which the politicians are very interested. The problems of obtaining finance are always receiving publicity, as are the number of business failures and liquidations. It is clearly a tricky area. Recently some of the banks have been installing microcomputers in a few test branches, presumably to determine whether or not the availability of financial modelling systems will enable them to make improved investment decisions by gaining a better understanding of the likely cash flow and profitability of their customers. This chapter includes some guidance on how to approach the banks and financial institutions when seeking money for a new venture, as it is considered that this will condition how the models are constructed and the results presented.

Cash flow forecasting in particular is important in most businesses but absolutely crucial for a new business start-up. Planning for this situation has to take account of the complexity of a pre-trading period in which the business is set up. It is here that decisions have to be made on the acquisition and financing of the assets of the business. Premises can be rented, leased or bought on a mortgage, and equipment can be acquired on lease or HP, or bought outright or secondhand. The product (if there is one) can be made from scratch or, to reduce the need for factory space and equipment, partly sub-contracted to other manufacturers.

Most microcomputer planning systems now contain features to aid investment decisions, such as discounted cash flow and payback period calculations. With or without these, the effects of different combinations of buy, lease and rent on debt repayments, cash flow, profit and balance sheet structure can be much more easily investigated on a computer-based system, taking the opportunity to try all the options. What follows describes one approach to the process and suggests the formats of suitable cash flow forecasts. If they are produced by a logical modeller, they can form the basis of creation of the logic files.

We approach the planning task as it relates to the starting of your own business by describing how to organise and present all the necessary information about your idea for a business and the company that will exploit it. 'Necessary for what?' you may ask. At first sight, this may not appear a particularly difficult task nor in itself to come really to the heart of the problems encountered when trying to go it alone. Our experience shows it to be highly relevant. Many discussions with people who want to start a business show that their ideas are not fully thought out and consequently are not described in a way which enables others, investors and bankers included, to understand them properly and see their full potential.

If you tackle the description of your idea and the initial planning of your business in the way outlined below, your chances of obtaining the required finance will be greatly increased. Not only that, you will have gained a head start on those who open up first and plan later (if at all), and also a greater understanding of any possible pitfalls and how to avoid them.

From the earlier chapters it will be clear that the work of planning a new business needs the aid of a financial modelling system as much as, if not more than, an existing business does. When nothing has yet started to happen, the feasible options of how to structure and operate the business are present in much greater numbers, and trying them all out - or at least a large number of them - is an ideal computer application.

Getting the Idea on Paper

Anyone seriously considering going it alone needs to have an idea of what sort of business he wants to enter. At the heart of any business with a future there are always products or services for which a market exists or can soon be developed. Once available for sale, however, the results of even the most innovative ideas tend to seem so obvious. Why, then, did we not all think of the 'Workmate', 'Oven Chips' or 'Speak'n Spell'? Perhaps it is not that easy to invent a winner.

One thing at least is clear. The product and its market are at all times inseparable. Anyone to whom you describe your idea - prospective partner, accountant, lawyer, banker, investor - will want to hear about both. What is more, they will expect you to know the answers to a large range of questions. No one will be very impressed if your replies include: 'I've been meaning to look into that' or 'I haven't worked it out yet'. After all, they will need to be convinced that you are (or will be) a competent businessman.

An obvious first step is to prepare a comprehensive definition of the idea itself. There is unlikely to be any alternative to writing it down but this is rarely as easy as first it seems. Initial enthusiasm for an idea is often short on the many points of detail on which its acceptability to others - and their ability to grasp its potential - stands or falls. A paradox of so-called 'going it alone' is the need to take all sorts of people with you.

Nevertheless, once complete, the definition will also serve as part of the required organised basis for the construction and input of the logic of a computer-based model.

Figure 6.1 should be read in conjuction with the remainder of this section. It is a checklist of the major points to consider on the product and its market. You will see that the following headings appear:

1. The product (or service) description.
2. Why it will sell.
3. Its intended market.
4. Its approximate selling price.
5. How it will be sold.
6. An estimate of sales volume.
7. How it will be made (or provided).
8. Its approximate cost.

The consideration of these points will inevitably raise some unresolved problems. What follows may help you to decide how to solve them and so assist in the completion of the planning sheet.

The product description

This is entirely your field, but take care to use only simple language, avoid jargon and difficult technical terms and describe it so that anyone can understand it. Be sure to say what it <u>does</u> and state the advantages of having or using it, as well as what it <u>is</u>. Be sure to say whether or not it is the subject of a patent.

Why it will sell

Here we are looking at what the marketing men call 'unique selling points' - USPs. These are often made as comparative statements, to bring out the contrast between the features of the new product and those currently on the market. At the simplest, you might be saying: 'People can now shop at my DIY centre instead of having to drive 50 miles to the only other one around here'. Alternatively, you may have a product that offers some or all of the features found in the competition, but at a far cheaper price (e.g. Cristal d'Arques glassware). Again, your product might perform better, have more features, last longer or cost less to run than others, while costing about the same. Where nothing directly comparable exists, it might fill a known need in a new way (e.g. Babygro) or alert people to a need of which they were previously unaware (e.g. bottled spa water, TV games).

The intended market

This has two dimensions - customer type and geographical. You might be aiming to sell to housewives under 40 in the north of England. You would need to find out through market research how many of them there were in that category and area. The very nature of the product may, if sufficiently specialised, define the customer group very closely (e.g. micro-circuits). Initially a revolutionary product may only be capable of appreciation by a small, technically aware group. Later it may be bought more widely (e.g. home hobby computers).

Most products are first marketed in their country of origin, unless designed specifically for overseas markets (e.g. tropical disease treatments). Sometimes a restricted sales area is chosen, either for the purposes of testing consumer reaction to the product or to keep down sales and distribution costs until profits

Figure 6.1   Checklist - product and market

Product description	What is it?
	What does it do?
	Attach sketch/photo if helpful
	Patent number
	No jargon
	Explain technical terms
Why it will sell	Cheaper
	Better availability in area
	Better features
	Lower running/maintenance costs
	Compare with other known products
Its intended market	Who it will appeal to in general
	Home market and source of market
	information
	Overseas possibilities and source
	of market information
	Planned initial sales area
	Total potential customers:
	initial area
	remainder of UK
	elsewhere
Its approximate selling price	How much will customers pay?
	Why?
	Differences: home; overseas
	Use average price if variable
	product (e.g. computer system)
How it will be sold	You as main salesman
	Salesforce
	To distributors, retailers, etc.
	Agents (where? what proportion?)
	Mail order, door-to-door
	Literature, manuals
	Advertising, promotion
An estimate of sales volume	Proportion of market
	Year by year for 3 years
	Initial market shown separately
	Exports kept separate
	Changes needed for different markets
How it will be made	Manufactured from raw materials
	Bought-in components
	Where assembled
	Licensed
	Sub-contracted
	Start one way, change later
Its approximate cost	Buying in costs for wholesaling
	See costing sheet for details
	Use today's value
	Cost small-value items in batch (say 100)
	Use average cost for variable product

start to build up. Alternatively, as in the example of the DIY centre above, the area in which sales will be made is intentionally local. Further relevant aspects of marketing are covered in more detail in many other publications on the subject.

Its approximate selling price

Many businesses, even old-established ones, make the major mistake of setting selling prices by 'cost plus' methods - working out what it costs to make the product and adding a percentage for 'profit'. This may be a suitable method for monopolies but in all other cases it ignores the crucial factor of what the customer is prepared to pay.

Be sure to price your product solely in the light of what you judge the market will bear. If you have discovered a way of turning water into petrol for 5p a gallon, you can be sure that it will still sell well at 10 per cent under current pump prices. On the other hand, merely because you have a product that costs you £10 to make is irrelevant if customers value it at about £5.

In your calculations of selling price you should (except for cash flow purposes in the following section) exclude VAT and other duties and taxes, as these will not accrue to the business but will have to be passed on to the tax man. In addition, remember that if you give discounts or sell through middlemen who take a commission, you will receive less in the end yourself from each sale.

How it will be sold

Customers can be alerted to a product's existence and benefits in a variety of ways, whose appropriateness depends both on its nature and the intended market. Door-to-door methods are sometimes suitable (e.g. Avon Cosmetics) as is mail order (e.g. Scotcade). Both these need the support of major advertising, which is difficult for most new small businesses to afford. Industrial and commercial products are often sold by some form of direct contact and demonstration, perhaps by technically trained sales staff and supported by descriptive literature or manuals. Often the boss of a small business will reserve the selling task to himself, unless his skills lie principally in other fields. The available selling methods include:

(a)   directly to the end-user by the manufacturer;
(b)   to distributors, wholesalers or retailers;
(c)   through agents;
(d)   via 'specifiers' (e.g. architects).

Most businesses in fact use a combination of methods, but for a new business it is as well to keep it as simple as possible. The method or combination of methods you will need to adopt depends on a variety of factors, not least the industry you are in.

Sometimes it can be more profitable (or perhaps the only practical solution) to sell the idea rather than the product based on it. 'Know-how' is normally sold by the granting of a licence in return for royalties on sales and/or a lump sum payment. In fact, the conditions can be virtually anything that the parties agree, and can include restriction on such things as the area in which sales may be made, the right to manufacture only, a licence for a set length of time and so on. Licensing can be the best course of action when:

(a)   the product is too complex for a small business or requires too much capital;

(b)   the product includes what the lawyers call 'intellectual property' (e.g. computer software);

(c)   the best way of entering certain markets is to allow companies already established there to manufacture and/or sell;

(d)   the product is not the sort of thing which would maintain your interest as the basis for a business;

(e)   you have other ideas that need financing and could use the money to greater effect.

An estimate of sales volume

From the section above on the intended market you have seen the need to identify the type and available number of customers for the product. Now is the time to estimate what proportion of them will actually buy it, year by year.

Of course, no question is more difficult than 'And how many do you think you can sell?', especially in the early years of a new business. Sales volume will be affected by selling price, selling methods, the ability of production to keep up with demand, not to mention the changing economic climate and the effect of government policy. Nevertheless, you <u>must</u> forecast what sales will be made in order to plan many crucial aspects of the business, including the need for working capital for such things as stocks, work-in-progress and debtors, and the amount of factory and storage space, plant and machinery that will be needed.

How it will be made

In order to offer a product for sale, it is not necessary to make anything yourself. Either by licensing or sub-contracting, all or part of the manufacturing can be done elsewhere, as can stockholding and even distribution. In such circumstances you would mainly concentrate on obtaining orders and thereafter on organising the roles of everyone else.

Alternatively, some components of the product may be available in standard form, and these can be bought in and assembled. Later you can consider manufacturing those components whose costs could be reduced or whose quality or continuity of supply could be better assured thereby. If the product is simple enough, you may be able to start by obtaining premises, plant and equipment (perhaps including secondhand items) and doing most of the manufacturing yourself.

Clearly, different approaches to producing the same product will result in different labour and material costs, need different amounts of working capital and investment in plant and lead to different levels of profit. Whatever methods you choose to begin with can be changed as sales increase and profits start coming in. The important thing is to start at a simple enough level and not try to do everything in-house from the first day of operation.

Its approximate cost

Here we deal with costs on a simplified basis by considering only the labour and materials which go into the product itself. Overheads are dealt with separately in the next section, on marginal costing principles - also called 'contribution accounting'. If this means nothing to you, you will need to refer to an appropriate book on the subject. If yours is to be a multi-product company, this part of the planning can be quite complex. If you are to be a wholesaler, your costs will simply be your buying-in prices. A costing sheet is included to help with your calculations. (See Figure 6.2)

Once you have worked out your costs, fill in the net selling price, excluding VAT and after discounts etc., and work out the material and labour content, each as a percentage of the selling price. The remaining percentage (to give a total of 100 per cent) is the gross profit per unit. As this has to pay for all the overheads and administrative expenses of the business, consider carefully whether or not it is adequate in view of the expected sales volumes.

Summary

You have now compiled a very comprehensive picture of your product and the market in which it will be sold. Seeing it all down on paper may cause you to make some amendments to your plans at this stage. For example, you may see that you need to find cheaper production methods or more sales to make for a profitable result.

The Financial Evaluation

The next step is to move on to a more financially based evaluation, which will lead to an estimate of the amount of money that will be needed for you to get started in business.

Anyone to whom you go with a proposal to finance your business will obviously ask 'How much do you want and what will you spend it on?' This section will help you to give a succinct but comprehensive answer in a form that an investor or banker will best understand, thereby giving you the best chance of obtaining the money.

You should be able to complete a great deal of the initial financial planning of the proposed business yourself. The most important part of this entails the drawing up of a forecast cash flow covering the period of formation of the business and its first few trading years. Figure 6.3 is a planning sheet which, as before, contains a checklist of items to consider. You should note, however, that a complete picture of the business will only be available when forecast profit and loss accounts and balance sheets have been drawn up, and it is here that you will probably require your accountant to help you. More sophisticated programs that address this area are becoming available for microcomputers, the one associated with MasterModeller being called Strategy Modeller.

The purpose of the planning sheet is not only to show how much cash is required but also what for and when. It will enable you to distinguish between requirements for working capital, for such things as stocks, work-in-progress and debtors; and money for fixed assets, such as buildings, plant and machinery. The planning sheet is intended to contain twenty columns, which, if each was to represent three months, would allow two formation years and the first three trading years to be covered. Other periods may be used if they are more appropriate in your case, but the remainder of the text assumes that quarters were selected. It is therefore in a suitable form for input to a financial planning system, but it is still a good idea to try it manually first of all, as this will highlight areas where modifications would better fit it to your particular circumstances.

Some lines on the planning sheet can clearly only be completed after separate calculations have been done elsewhere. Production wages and materials (lines 6 and 7) are examples of this and, depending on the complexity of your business,

Figure 6.2   Costing sheet

	£
Its approximate cost	
Bought-in components	
Raw materials	
Labour hours, raw material to components Total hours ..... @ £ ...../hr =	
Sub-contracted tasks	
Assembly materials	
Assembly labour, ... hours @ £ ...../hr =	
Testing and inspection, ... hours @ £ ...../hr =	
Average rectification per unit	
Packing materials	
Packing labour, ... hours @ £ ...../hr =	
Delivery (if included)	
Other costs	
TOTAL COST PER UNIT	

Net sales value £ ....

Total labour £ ....   Total material £ ....

.....% labour   .....%material   .....%gross profit

Figure 6.3   Planning sheet - cash flow

Period start dates (period length .... mths)		
1 Sales units (units used ....)		
2 Net sales value inc. VAT		
3 Receipts from debtors		
4 Other income		
5 Total receipts		
6 Direct wages inc. NHI/pensions		
7 Direct materials inc. VAT		
8 Direct consumables		
9 Production mgt/supv. sals		
10 Indirect wages (production)		
11 Machinery maintenance/spares		
12 Factory maintenance		
13 Transport/handling equipment		
14 Factory light/power/heat		
15 Factory rent/rates		
16 Sales salaries + commissions		
17 Bad debts		
18 Sales travel/entertainment		
19 Advertising/promotion		
20 Admin./clerical sals		
21 Office rent/rates		
22 Office heat/light/power		
23 Telephone/postage		
24 Insurance		
25 Office building maintenance		
26 Office equipment maintenance		
27 Printing/stationery		
28 Cleaning		
29 Directors/managers salaries		
30 Dir./man. travel/expenses		
31 Pensions (not national scheme)		
32 Purchase of fixed assets (TOTAL: £ .....)		
33 Lease/HP factory equipment		
34 Lease/HP office equipment		
35		
36		
37		
38		
39		
40 Cash out		
41 Capital repayments		
42 Interest payments		
43 Total cash out		
44 Cash in (line 3, later line 5)		
45 Cash out (line 40, later line 43) - cash in		
46 Cumulative cash required		

59

there may be others. The logic file might be able to include these calculations. To proceed, you will now need to construct an appropriate logic file to produce the repeat format in Figure 6.2, and then print out a worksheet on which to enter the figures. It would be best, however, to read the next sections before starting this work, to ensure that all the required features are included.

Sales revenue

Begin by filling in the dates of the quarters along the top and drawing a vertical line before the column that represents the first quarter in which the first invoiced sales will be made. Next, divide the sales forecast you made in the last section into quarters, allowing for seasonal variations, and enter it on line 2, starting at the vertical line. Space is allowed on line 1 for sales units to be entered if required but this will not be possible with a multi-product company unless some convenient global measure exists (e.g. weight). This time VAT should be added to the net sales value after discounts and commissions. Do not worry about the effects of inflation - work out everything at today's prices and costs, no matter how far into the future. The computer-based system will let you include the inflationary element later.

   As this is a cash flow, you now have to estimate how long it will take people to pay for the sales you have invoiced. These days that may be two to three months later. To allow for this delay, offset the amounts on line 2 in one column to the right and fill them in on line 3, 'receipts from debtors'. MasterModeller includes an offsetting feature for exactly this purpose. For now, leave lines 4 and 5 blank.

Financing the fixed assets

Now come the 'cash out' calculations, which are far more lengthy. This section covers the money for the acquisition of items which may form part of the company's fixed assets. To decide whether or not they will, you must choose how to finance them. A factory can be rented and plant and machinery acquired on lease or HP. Secondhand equipment, though, normally has to be bought outright. You may already own some of these items. The checklist allows space for you to list the items you need, together with their approximate costs and an indication of whether you will buy, rent, lease or use HP. As a rough guide, leasing costs (at the time of writing) are in the region of £70 per £1000 leased per quarter over five years.

   Having selected those items that you will buy outright (even on borrowed money), you can fill in the amounts for their purchase in the appropriate columns on line 32. Note that there is also space at the extreme left for the total costs of all such items. Lease and HP payments go on lines 15 and 21 and property rents as part of the total figures which make up lines 33 and 34.

Other expenditure

You can now move on to the remaining 'cash out' items. These comprise the costs of making the product and the expenses of running the company. Collectively, your suppliers will make up your creditors and one method of raising money is to delay their payment. They will be unlikely, however, to allow you much credit in your early period of trading, and you will need to build up their confidence in you by paying promptly; so it is probably better to show the cash as going out in the period in which the purchases are made rather than to offset it, as in the case of sales revenue.

Direct costs

Lines 6 to 8 relate to the labour and material that go into the product. Your costings from the previous section will give you the basis of the values to enter, as percentages of the sales figures on line 2. Obviously, though, you cannot have 10 per cent of a machine operator. Similarly, materials normally come in minimum purchase lots - you cannot have a single bolt or micro-circuit. Thus the labour and material values will have to take account of the realities of employment and purchasing should add 30 per cent to these direct labour costs and all other salaries and wages to cover NHI and pension contributions.

Indirect costs

Last of all, fill in the indirect costs and administrative expenses on lines 9 to 39 by reference to the checklist, and make a sub-total of all the 'cash out' items on line 40. You are still lacking the information needed to calculate the capital and interest repayments on lines 41 and 42, but, as these depend on the amount and method of any borrowing, which itself is only revealed by the cash flow calculations on lines 44 to 46, these have to be completed first, and the logic must be written to allow for them to be worked out last of all.

Initial cash flow calculation

For this next calculation we need to go back to the 'cash out' sub-total on line 40. From this, and the sales receipts on line 3, you can now calculate the cash flow summary on lines 44 to 46, as shown in the example. This shows the total amount of cash that the business needs, cumulatively quarter by quarter. Normally it gives negative values throughout the period of formation and early trading, when payments usually exceed receipts. Apart from lease and HP finance, which has already been calculated, you now have to consider where to find the remainder.

This normally comes from a combination of your own resources and amounts of long- and short-term borrowing. Working capital is normally considered short-term and is financed by bank overdraft. Long-term borrowing and equity is normally related to fixed assets, as they are likely to have a long life, but can also be appropriate to any 'hard core' working capital which does not fluctuate greatly. Space is given to make a note of the amount of each type of finance that will be used. If you cannot provide adequate security for the type and amount of borrowing that you need, you will, in effect, be asking the lenders to share a proportion of the risk. In return for this, they will be likely to wish to acquire a proportion of the equity in the business.

You now have enough information to approach the banks and financial institutions for the money you need. Once you have finalised your borrowing arrangements, you can input the amounts to be received from the lenders (together with the money you will contribute yourself) on the 'other income' line (4), and the interest and capital repayments on line 4 and rework the cash flow. In its new form it will show the intended level of the bank overdraft, quarter by quarter. The model will, of course, work perfectly well without this data for a 'first run'.

Figure 6.4   Checklist - cash flow

Sales and   Calculate a net sales value after discounts
cash in   etc
                  Only salesman's commission is separate
                  (part of line 16).
                  Add VAT to the net sales value.
                  Other income (line 4) is for amounts
                  borrowed and your own contributions -
                  leave till last.
                  Total receipts (line 5) - leave till last.

Cash out   Add 30 per cent to all salary and wage
             amounts for NHI and pensions.
                  Direct wages (line 6) is calculated as a
                  percentage of sales value ex VAT as per
                  your product costings and adjusted to
                  'whole people'.
                  Direct materials (line 7) ditto but
                  include VAT on the calculated amount for
                  materials and adjust to allow for initial
                  stocking and available purchase lot quan-
                  tities.
                  Items on lines 9 to 15 include warehouse
                  items as well as factory.
                  Advertising/promotion not to include
                  manuals, operating instructions etc. -
                  use line 27.
                  Transport/handling (line 13) to include
                  fork lifts etc. running costs, not pur-
                  chase/lease or HP.
                  Travel/entertainment (lines 18 and 30)
                  to include car-running costs, not
                  purchase, lease or HP.
                  Before filling in lines 32, 33 and 34,
                  fill in checklist at extreme right of
                  planning sheet.

             See worked example on reverse before
             attempting.
Cash flow   Use pencil first time.
                  Calculation done in two stages, before and
                  after arranging borrowing.

                  First calculation reveals total cash needs.
                  Second calculation includes costs of
                  borrowing.

                  Line 46 is a progressive addition of the
                  amounts on line 45, column by column.

                  After second calculation, amounts in line
                  46 represent moving value of overdraft/
                  cash in hand.

Revising the cash flow

Things seldom work out exactly as planned, and so the task of keeping the cash flow up-to-date will be almost continuous. You would also be sensible to inform your bankers and investors as early as possible of any problems revealed by the changing cash flow. However difficult the circumstances, they will always be more likely to support you if they are told in advance rather than left to find out when the crisis has materialised. You will, after all, have demonstrated that you are well in touch with what is going on. Once the business is operating, cash control will be a vital management task, especially in the early years of trading.

Conclusion

In this chapter we have aimed to demonstrate that, in order to get started in business on your own, you must do as much detailed thinking and planning in advance as possible. If you have had the opportunity to complete the planning sheets on MasterModeller or a similar system, we hope that they will have enabled you to firm up on the detail of any business ideas you may have had. Thereafter, use of a microcomputer planning system will enable the plans to be refined and the best option selected. Perhaps you will have come across some aspects that may previously have been insufficiently thought out or possibly even forgotten altogether. You will certainly have assembled enough information to convince investors and others that you are serious and knowledgeable about starting your own business or your new project and, in so doing, will also have convinced yourself of the soundness or not of your idea to start a business.

Chapter 7
PLANNING NEEDING OTHER SOLUTIONS

Apart from using a microcomputer to aid in planning, the other main way of harnessing the power of computers to the task is to acquire planning packaged software for a larger computer, often one already installed in the company.

Large Computer Package

This is a sensible route where one or more of the following applies:

(a)   there is already a computer installation serving (or extendable to serve) those who would need to use the planning system;

(b)   more than one user will require regular access to the planning system;

(c)   users will want to use the same models and data;

(d)   the planning process will be extensively based on data already stored in the computer.

Such packages are readily available for the types of computer that are most widely sold, but can be expensive, costing up to £25,000 for the most sophisticated on the market.

Computer-based packages for minicomputers and mainframes are much more powerful than most microcomputer planning systems, particularly as they utilise the large capacity 'hard' disks found on these machines to make such things as consolidations and complex matrix handling very fast and almost completely automatic. It is also much easier to implement workable interfaces between the packages and data already on the computer in, say, the accounting system, than on microcomputers. This is partly because larger installations tend to have specialist staff in attendance to help with such problems but also because more help is forthcoming from the suppliers as higher value sales are concerned.

In summary, it is always a good idea to explore the nature of the need for computer-based planning systems in an organisation before deciding which solution

- micro or packages on larger systems - will be appropriate. Often it is not just a case of simple cost comparison, but rather the identification of the source of the methods and facilities that are needed to do the job properly.

Part II

Introduction

The purpose of this part is to examine the microprocessor used as the basis of a microcomputer business system. It has been written as far as possible in non-technical terms and is intended primarily for someone who, while contemplating a computerised business system for the first time, wants to know more about the workings of the computer itself and how to go about selecting and buying appropriate hardware and software.

What is a Microcomputer?

First of all it is worth defining what it is that makes a computer a microcomputer. The answer is that the function of processing information is carried out on any computer by what is called the 'central processing unit' (CPU). Most CPUs are now made on a single integrated circuit chip and it is this that is known as a microprocessor. Any computer with a microprocessor as its CPU is called a microcomputer.

It is this advance in technology that has meant that microcomputer systems are available at very low costs and with computing power equivalent to systems ten times the physical size and costing ten times the price five years ago. What happened to the electronic calculator has now also happened to commercial computing systems.

However, a computer system is more than just a calculator and its installation can have a profound effect upon a business. The amount of money spent on a microcomputer system initially may be small, and hence the risk of wasting money is less in the event of the system not working. But the disruption that the failure of a system can cause can be severe. For example, unreconciled accounts, incorrect invoices or delayed printing of statements can result in a serious financial loss.

It is therefore important to have a basic understanding of the normal elements of a microcomputer business system and their limitations. It is equally important that, armed with this understanding, you go about the process of determining the feasibility in your particular circumstances and the purchase of a microcomputer in the right way.

All computers have four basic functions:

(a)   input of information;
(b)   processing of information;
(c)   storage of information;
(d)   output of information.

In any form of business computer these four functions are carried out by various pieces of equipment (usually referred to as hardware) put together to form the total system. The system is controlled by programs (usually called software), which themselves fall into two main categories. One type, usually referred to as the 'operating system', controls the actual functioning of the hardware, together with the way it controls, schedules and manages the work it has to do. The other category is that of the application programs, which allow the computer to perform the particular jobs that it is doing (for example, payroll or stock control). We shall look at each of these four functions on a microcomputer by referring to the elements of a typical microcomputer system.

The Elements of a Microcomputer Business System

Below we study the four functions in detail while at the same time describing the equipment used to perform each one.

Input

Input of information to a business microcomputer is through a keyboard laid out in the standard typewriter format. It is appropriate in many business applications for this keyboard to include a separate numeric keypad in calculator format to speed up purely numeric entry. This keyboard is usually part of a unit containing a visual display, like a television screen, on which the operator can be prompted for entry by the computer and see the data being displayed as it is keyed in. In such a form it is normally referred to as a visual display unit or VDU. In the case of many of the cheaper 'do-it-yourself' home microcomputer assemblies it will be suggested that you make use of old TV sets for display purposes.

The fact that the keyboard is laid out in a standard typewriter format and that the better written standard application programs can prompt the operator with straightforward messages such as 'Enter employee number', 'Enter basic hours', means that the systems are usually easy to use and do not require any specially trained personnel. As most business applications deal with mainly numeric entry, typing ability is not usually essential either.

Processing

Processing on a microcomputer, as we have already discussed, is carried out by the microprocessor, the 'brains' of the system. The microprocessor has two functions to perform:

(a)   to control the operation of the computer;
(b)   to carry out logical and arithmetic operations on the data held in the computer.

It carries out these functions in two ways. The first is done by the use of the operating system, which is normally held permanently in the computer's memory and defines how the various pieces of equipment on the computer should function. The second uses the particular application program that is running, e.g. payroll, and this is only stored in the memory of the computer while it is actually being worked upon.

The processor carries out the sequence of instructions specified in the program. In so doing, it performs all the arithmetic operations and manipulation of data required.

There are a large number of 'package' programs available for common business applications such as ledger accounting and payroll, i.e. programs that are not written specifically for one company's requirements but are offered for sale in a standard form. These programs are relatively inexpensive and usually offer the advantage of being error-free and, from the better suppliers, well documented.

If an application is specially written to your requirements, or modifications are made to a standard program to achieve the same objective, the costs will be much greater. It is also worth noting that these costs are likely to continue to increase sharply over the next few years as they are mainly dependent upon programmer labour rates. This will have two results. Firstly the cost of programs on a typical system is likely to equal or even exceed the costs of the equipment itself. Secondly, to set against this, a much wider selection of standard programs is now available and companies will be more prepared to compromise on their requirements and accept standard programs as the cost advantage of so doing becomes increasingly attractive.

This may also prompt some people to consider writing their own programs, and most commercial microcomputer systems are designed so that they can be programmed directly. Programs are written in various 'languages', which are sets of instructions such as 'multiply', 'divide', 'store', or in some instances the equivalent code for these demands.

The most common language used on commercial microcomputers is BASIC, which, as the name suggests, is an elementary, relatively simple language to learn. PASCAL is another language, which is now popular and is widely used in further educational establishments to teach and promote structured programming skills. However, most purchasers are not concerned with what language is used so long as their system carries out the job that it was bought for!

The size of the memory determines the complexity of the programs that can be run and the amount of input, storage and output equipment that can be handled to complete the system.

Storage

There are two types of storage on a microcomputer. First comes 'memory', where the programs and data that the processor is currently using are resident, and, second, other media, where programs and data can be stored long term for future use.

Memory is split into ROM (read only memory), where information is written during the manufacturing process and cannot be altered, and RAM (random access memory), where information can be entered into or retrieved from any storage position. Microprocessors are available in a variety of designs, some of which will have amounts of ROM and/or RAM on the same chip. More usually, some or all of these types of memory are provided by separate chips mounted on the same board as the microprocessor, whose function is dedicated to memory alone.

The ROM memory will, where the operating system is designed into the micro-circuitry as opposed to being in the form of a conventional program, provide this and certain other fixed functions. These will often come into effect automatically as soon as the computer is switched on (called 'bootstrapping') and will, for example, allow you the routines to load the particular application program that you decide to work on. Without these 'wired-in' functions (or alternatively the user keying in instructions to call the operating system), the computer would be inoperable. The RAM memory will hold the application programs and data that you are currently working on.

Memory sizes are usually quoted in 'K', (e.g. 512K) where K usually stands for 1000 bytes. A byte is roughly equivalent to an alpha or numeric character. A 512K processor therefore means a processor with a capacity of 512,000 characters. Of this capacity, perhaps a small part would be used up by the operating system, leaving the rest for the application program and any data that the program has to work on (and therefore has to be temporarily stored). An application program can be of almost any size, depending on the complexity of the task it has to perform and the skill of the programmer in using the minimum number of instructions to obtain the required results.

It is obviously vital to ensure that the system you buy has a large enough memory for the job that you wish to run, so some evidence of programs of a similar complexity to your own requirement should be asked for from any potential computer suppliers.

Unless information is to be keyed in every time an application is to run, programs and data have to be stored for future use and therefore must be held on other media designed for this purpose. The two most common types are flexible diskettes ('floppy disks') and hard disks ('Winchester disks').

Cassettes (similar to music cassettes) are the normal method of program loading and storage used on the home 'personal' microcomputers that are now being sold in the High Street for £100-£1000. The cassettes themselves are cheaper than flexible diskettes and the cassette drive, often simply a domestic cassette recorder/player, is much cheaper than a purpose-designed diskette drive unit. They are, however, much slower, because the cassette must be read sequentially to access any piece of information held on it, whereas the diskette offers direct access to any data stored on it, making use of some kind of automatically created index.

This makes the cassette unsuitable for most commercial applications where information records usually have to be accessed at random. For example, sales invoicing from stock would require access to customer account and stock records in any order, unless a great deal of manual pre-sorting of information had been carried out. Even if this was attempted, it is difficult to see how both the customers and the stock items could be simultaneously in sequence. Payroll is probably the only major commercial application where records can easily be processed in sequential order.

More common for business systems are the 'floppy disks', which come in three sizes, 3½", 5¼" or 8" diameter, and look like the 45RPM records that are sent through the post. There is random access to information held on floppy disk, i.e. any data record can be retrieved immediately without having to go through the whole disk, which accounts for its greater speed. Producing a list of debtors with aged balances would be simply a matter of inserting the sales ledger disk into the machine and starting the program. This is therefore a major benefit over both the sequential access cassette and the old fashioned visible record systems, where all the information is held on cards which have to be selected and hand-fed into the machine.

The amount that one floppy disk can store ranges from 80,000 to 1,000,000 (commonly referred to as a 'megabyte', written 'Mb') characters of information, the difference relating mainly to the way in which the manufacturer has designed the arrangement and density of the magnetically stored information. To put this into perspective, one sales ledger account or employee record might take up about 250 characters. Most microcomputer business systems will have a floppy disk unit and a hard disk. This makes it a simple matter for the contents of a disk to be copied on to blank disks for security purposes.

Most microcomputer systems utilise hard disks with a capacity of 10-30 Mb upwards, which are far more expensive. This type of sealed unit hard disk, called a 'Winchester' disk, after the IBM location in the USA at which it was first developed, is now the norm. These are much faster in accessing records and can be used either when one application requires more than can be held on diskette or when several applications are required to be stored at the same time, and where again this is beyond the capacity of a diskette-only system.

The use of magnetic storage on diskettes or disks thereby results in most circumstances in a fundamental change in record storage from a visible (loose-leaf or card) system to an invisible one. This can be a cause of some concern to people used to more traditional visible systems but that concern should prove unwarranted, as the information should be equally accessible, either on the VDU or in printed form, e.g. copy statements to check cash received. It does mean, however, that care should be taken over the security of data stored. Master record diskettes should be copied on a daily basis and the copies kept in a separate location from the masters.

Output

We have already seen that information produced by the microcomputer can be provided either in display form on the VDU or by being printed. There is a wide range of printers available both in terms of quality and speed, from a basic 20 characters per second printer to the much more expensive line printers with speeds up to 400 lines per minute or more and now laser printers of up to twelve A4 pages per minute. The majority of printers used on small business systems are of the dot-matrix type. If a higher quality of print is required, perhaps for letter-writing when the computer is also undertaking word processing, a more expensive daisy-wheel or laser printer, which can produce to typewriter standard, would be needed. These normally print at 40 to 60 characters per second compared to the common matrix printers at 150 to 200 characters per second. Some of the matrix printers have two or more speeds, immediately selectable by the user, allowing quality to be sacrificed for faster output where appropriate.

The Complete System

If we put these four functions of input, processing, storage and output together into a typical microcomputer business system configuration it would look like Figure II.1.

The 'bus' is a common path along which all data and instructions move to and from each part of the system. Some bus structures allow you to increase the size of the system by adding more memory or interfaces through simply plugging in extra circuit boards. The choice of a system that uses one of the standard bus structures ensures this greater flexibility for the future. An interface is a microelectronic device (sometimes in the form of an additional chip, sometimes part of the microprocessor) which allows information to move backwards and forwards between the CPU and the external peripherals such as the floppy disks or the printer.

To give a practical example of the above microcomputer system, let us assume that it is being used by a company to process sales ledger, purchase ledger and payroll. The program instructions to perform these three functions and the main data files (the sales and purchase ledger accounts and employee records) would be held permanently on the diskettes. If we want to post some cash received to various sales ledger accounts, we would type in the name of that routine on the keyboard of our VDU. This would cause the cash received program to be copied from the floppy disk to the RAM memory. We would then enter the first sales account number that we wished to access and that account record would also be moved from disk to RAM memory. The amount of cash would be entered, the sales account balances updated accordingly and the record finally be moved back to the floppy disk in its new form. The next account number would be entered and the process repeated for all cash received.

If, after this, we then wanted to do the weekly payroll, we would type in the name of the payroll routine. This would cause the sales cash received program to be moved back to the disk and the payroll program to be moved from disk to RAM memory.

Figure II.1 **Microcomputer business system configuration**

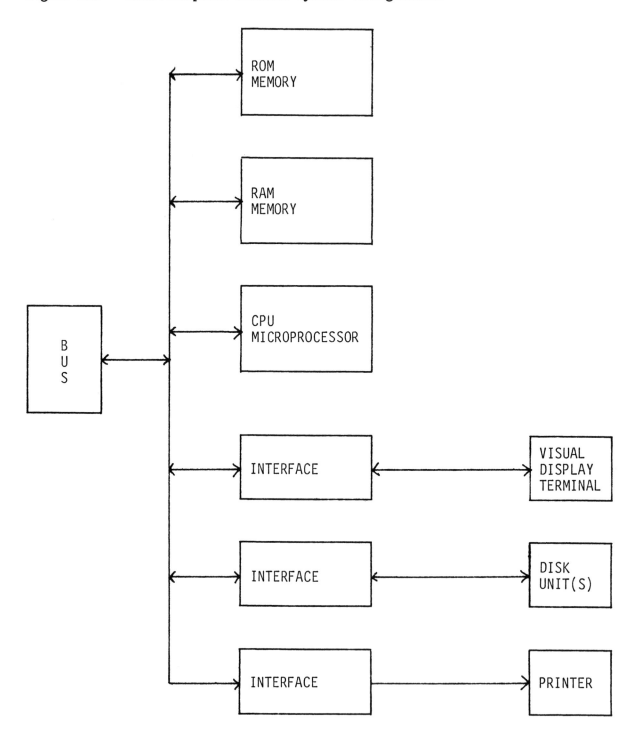

Figure II.2 Payroll routine

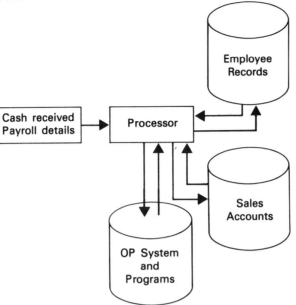

Figure II.2 summarises the process. It can be seen that the floppy disks hold the information permanently, while the memory only holds the programs and records that it is currently working on.

Some microcomputers, provided that the processor is big enough and that the operating system is designed to handle it, and given that all the required programs and information are all on the disks or diskettes at the same time, can perform more than one program simultaneously. This ability would allow the concurrent running of two or more routines, e.g. payroll calculation and sales ledger postings, but would obviously also require further visual display units to be attached and would thereby increase the cost of the system. The capacity speed at which information on a diskette can be accessed is not sufficient to make this a workable solution, so that a hard disk will be necessary as well. Typical microcomputers capable of providing these "multi-processing" facilities can be expanded up to 6, 8 or more VDUs depending upon the size of the processor and its ability to cope with the workload.

A further development in microcomputers is the introduction of networking techniques, where two or more microcomputers are linked together. Each user in the network has a VDU and processor, which has access to shared hard disk units and printers. This approach allows a large number of VDUs to be linked together, providing access to many sources of information within a company. Special multi-user programmes are required to enable this technique to be employed.

Where Does the Microcomputer Fit into the Computer Range?

There are basically three types of computer:

(a)   microcomputer (including 'personal' computers);
(b)   minicomputer;
(c)   mainframe.

It is difficult to define the difference between a micro and a minicomputer. At its smallest, the minicomputer is very similar in power, operation and cost to the micro. However at present minicomputer systems are distinguished mainly by their ability to be expanded by the addition of further memory, communications facilities, printers and VDUs to a far greater extent than micros, to systems costing well over £500,000. How long this difference will last remains to be seen.

The mainframe computer is a large, immensely powerful computer requiring a special air-conditioned environment, normally a data processing department to support it and costing upwards of £500,000. It is used to process large amounts of data on a number of simultaneous jobs, either fed into it directly or from a network of other microcomputers or minicomputers.

How Can a Microcomputer Help?

The microcomputer can be used to help in many aspects of the smaller business, for example:

Sales

(a) Processing of sales orders, producing the necessary paperwork for such things as picking from stock and despatch control.
(b) Highlighting overdue orders, producing invoices.
(c) Producing analyses of sales and profitability by customer and product.

Accounting

(a) Incomplete records applications as part of audit work.
(b) Maintaining the sales, purchase and nominal ledgers.
(c) Producing fee accounts from time records in professional firms.
(d) Producing monthly statements and aged lists of debtors.
(e) Producing cheques, remittance advices and aged lists of creditors.
(f) Producing trial balances, profit and loss statements and the balance sheet.

Payroll

Calculation of the weekly and monthly payroll with automatic tax and NI contribution calculation. Producing P60s.

Production

(a) Control of stock levels against demand.
(b) Control of work-in-progress.

Costing

Up-to-date costing and profitability of operations, processes, jobs or contracts.

Word Processing

An increasing area of interest to small businesses, word processing is the manipulation of text by computer, which is particularly useful in such applications as report writing, mail-shot sales letters and sales proposals. Reports can be produced in draft, then easily amended and reproduced. The same standard letters can be sent to a list of customers, with each letter appearing to be specially written. Standard paragraphs can be held and manipulated for the swift production of contracts and agreements.

If used for word processing, a commercial microcomputer system will normally require a high quality printer to be attached if it is intended that some or all of the output is sent to customers. This could easily increase the cost of the system by £2000, which could well be as much or more than the rest of the equipment combined.

Microcomputers are available with package programs which facilitate word processing, though frequently without the simplified function control offered by the labelled control keys of purpose-built word processors (e.g. 'insert', 'delete', 'copy').

How Do You Select the Correct Computer System?

There are two main reasons for changing from a manual to a computerised system. The first is that the volume of data to be processed is such that either it will be impossible to continue to process it manually or it will only be possible by recruiting further staff. The second reason is that the complexity of the data to be processed or the information and analysis required is such that it cannot be done adequately by the existing staff.

If either of these conditions exists there could, depending upon the cost, be justification for some type of computer system. Nevertheless, far too many companies rush into computerisation without justification, perhaps because it is considered 'the thing to do' or because they come across a particularly persuasive computer salesman.

If you think there is justification, forget about computer equipment itself. The first step is to decide what you are going to require the computer to do on each function where it might be employed. Write down in detail what you plan to key into this system, what you are going to store, and what information you want out and in what form. You need not worry how the system will actually carry this out internally.

If you do this for each function you wish to computerise (e.g. fee accounting, sales order processing, payroll, etc.) and you also work out carefully the volumes of data (e.g. number of sales orders to be entered each day and number of items on each) and include these, you should end up with what is usually called a specification of your computing requirements.

The preparation of this specification requires a great deal of effort, but, if it is done correctly, it can prevent many problems and mistakes later. Depending upon the complexity of the requirements, it is often helpful to use an independent third party to assist you in this task, someone with experience of system design who can ensure that you have covered every aspect.

Common Problems of Computerisation

Unrealistic timescales

Computer installations often do not achieve their full potential or, worse still, fail completely, because unrealistic timescales are set for their implementation. As a rough guide you should allow the following periods, from signing contracts with a supplier to achieving fully operating systems:

(a)   Simple accounts or stock recording, 6-9 months.
(b)   Complex distribution or production control, 12-36 months.

Both the above timescales are based on experience of implementing standard software only, with little or no modification other than laying out the required formats for printed reports. Projects that include any significant writing of special programs will normally take considerably longer.

Inadequately defining the problem

Too often approaches are made to suppliers of computer hardware or services when the real business problems to be solved are still not defined in any detail. The result of any such approach to suppliers invariably results in their producing a 'quick quotation'. Suppliers, not unnaturally, work towards an early contact with a prospective buyer in a variety of ways - through exhibitions, demonstrations, publicity material and trade magazines. As a result of such initial contacts, the prospective purchaser will be invited to describe in broad terms how he believes he could make use of a computer. After this, a quotation will be received.

Accepting a quotation given against a general statement of requirements is not a recipe for success, as the descriptive terms used are, even with the best of intentions by both supplier and customer, subject to a very wide range of meanings and interpretation. For example, your view of what constitutes a comprehensive stock control or accounting system may differ from the salesman's and he will rarely have as much expertise as his customer in the customer's type of business or speciality. It is therefore essential for accurate communication between customer and supplier that systems requirements are specified with precision and this means in writing. A checklist of what to include appears in Appendix 1.

Obsolete hardware

Hardware manufacturers are continually announcing new products. In attempting to assess products or services available there is therefore always the worry that a technological breakthrough is just around the corner and will render obsolescent any system just acquired.

There is no completely foolproof method of avoiding this eventuality. It is more a question of weighing up the advantages to be gained by computerisation now against the benefit of possibly improved technology in say a year or so, keeping track of general trends in equipment design and development and asking specific questions about the date of original introduction, latest modification and so on of the equipment you actually intend to buy. As in the case of every investment decision, if there are savings to be made immediately and the purchase makes sense financially, it is better to be making what savings you can than waiting for the opportunity to make greater savings at some unspecified time in the future.

Software pitfalls

It is important to appreciate that there is no fixed relationship between the cost of a computer and the cost of the software required for a company's systems. Standard programs or packages are generally to be preferred where available, as they cost only a fraction of specially developed and written ones. A snag with standard programs is that, particularly in the case of those available for microcomputers and the way in which they tend to be offered for sale, they are often bought on the basis of a general description in a supplier's catalogue. Too often they do not work as well as anticipated, and contain omissions which cannot be detected simply from general discussion. It is therefore essential to ensure that any decision to buy software is based on detailed demonstration of its use.

Additionally, such demonstrations will be far more meaningful if undertaken by another customer who is actually using the software, rather than in a supplier's office. In the latter case the software is set up for demonstration purposes with data files containing only a small proportion of the information that a working system would have to hold, thereby giving an unrepresentative performance.

With special tailor-made software there is the danger of the programs being developed on the basis of insufficiently detailed definition. Costs - and the timescale - increase as necessary modifications and additions are carried out.

An added difficulty arises where separate contracts are negotiated with hardware and software suppliers. With this split responsibility it can be difficult to get redress in a situation of system malfunction or failure to achieve desired results.

The implementation of a computer system is therefore a complex undertaking to the extent that only when a specification has been completed are you in a position to know exactly what the system should do, how much data storage is required, how much information has to be keyed in daily and how much has to be printed out.

Having been through the difficult part, you can think about where you might get a computer system to meet your specification. This book is primarily concerned with microcomputer systems. It may of course be the case that your specification reveals that a minicomputer is needed, or that use of a bureau would be more appropriate.

Types of Supplier

There are several quite distinct types of supplier in the computer market:

(a)   hardware manufacturer;
(b)   software (or systems) house;
(c)   shop.

It is vitally important when considering computerisation that the special features of each type are understood. Below is a brief guide to what each offers and their special strengths and weaknesses.

Hardware manufacturer

This supplier is in business to sell computer hardware and any advice he gives will be oriented towards this end. He may offer some application packages as an incentive to buy equipment. These packages are usually well proven and have comprehensive documentation. The manufacturer will not necessarily undertake to modify packages to requirements or to write special programs. Moreover, unless the manufacturer's salesman knows that he has direct competition, he is less likely to be concerned to offer you the most cost-effective model in the range.

Points in favour of dealing directly with manufacturers are that they are usually more financially stable than software houses and can offer better support. They have experience in a variety of industries and should be able to arrange visits to other users in the area. It is, however, extremely unlikely that a manufacturer of microcomputers will deal directly with its end customers, unless of course, very large numbers of machines are to be bought.

Some manufacturers are happy to take complete responsibility for your computerisation project. Others insist on a separate agreement with a software house for any customised programs required - almost inevitably giving rise to the 'two contracts' problem. The danger in such a case is that if the system does not work each supplier can blame the other, which is of no help to the purchaser.

Software (or systems) house

Most software houses started in business by specialising in the provision of custom-written programs for unusual applications. Now they may offer some program packages (usually derived from previous work for customers) and be willing to modify these if necessary.

Successful software houses can offer very specialised experience if your requirements match work they have already tackled. They are, however, not totally impartial and although their salesmen may be called 'consultants', they have an understandable incentive to persuade you towards their services and the type of hardware of which they have experience.

Many software houses offer 'turnkey deals' in which they undertake to provide hardware and develop the software to a stage where you and your staff can step in and take over the running of the system. Such arrangements overcome the 'two contracts' problem - you can insist that the software house is responsible for any failures in performance - but there is still an absolute requirement for comprehensive specification of what is to be achieved and day-to-day participation and control.

Software houses tend to attract technically competent staff but you should still be aware of the importance of their providing you with good documentation at every stage of development. Even the best staff can change jobs, and you do not want to have to foot the bill while a junior programmer picks his way through the coding written by the genius who left last Friday.

Systems houses which have started up in business more recently have had the benefit of being able to become agents for ranges of microcomputers and package software, and only some of them have thought it appropriate to develop the ability to modify packages or write special programs.

Shops

Most people will have noticed that there are now High Street shops where computer equipment and programs can be bought. While some of these will have characteristics of software or systems houses, in that they have in-depth understanding of the application of the products they sell to business situations, many will concentrate mainly on the technical aspects of the systems they sell. They will be able to supply equipment with, in most cases, certain standard programs, e.g. sales ledger. The drawback to this approach is that the shop is primarily concerned with selling equipment, and the purchaser is often left to arrange for any special programming himself. Writing a complete set of programs oneself is both time-consuming and difficult, despite what one might be led to believe from sales literature. Most company managers would not have the necessary time available. Such shops will, however, be likely to offer very keen prices and so, if support is not an essential criterion, they may be the best form of supplier. A key point is to make sure that, at the very least, the supplier is in a position to offer and provide a comprehensive maintenance service for the equipment.

Summary

The two main ways of buying a microcomputer are therefore either direct from a shop or through a third party systems or software company. If the intending user is not prepared to write programs and so has to contract with a third party to do this, there may be a 'two contract' problem, where, should there be a system failure either the equipment or the programs (or both) could be blamed.

The sensible approach for most companies contemplating the purchase of a system for the first time is to go to a systems company. These companies buy in equipment from the manufacturer, program it to a particular requirement and then sell the complete system to the end user. The result is usually, at least at first sight, thought to be rather more expensive than buying direct but is more likely to result in a workable, better-supported system, with the responsibility resting on one supplier.

It is not possible to give any accurate guidelines as to the cost of microcomputer business systems, as this will depend upon the functions they are intended to cover and the volumes of data to be processed. To give a rough idea of prices, a complete set of equipment for a single user system can currently cost anything from £1500 to £15,000 and individual programs from £40 to £5000 or more.

Getting Quotations

Theoretically it would be possible to contact every manufacturer and software house listed in the <u>Computer Users Yearbook</u> and <u>Computing Marketplace</u>. However, processing quotations is time-consuming and a manageable number for a small system is at the most five or six. Even with this number you may obtain only three serious contenders in the final analysis. Looking at it from the suppliers' point of view, and remembering that the 'grapevine' in the computer business is very good and your requirement for a system will probably be widely known in your locality, they will not want to feel they only have a one in ten chance of getting any business. If this was to be the case, you could hardly expect them to spend a lot of time and trouble on your quotation.

The first step, therefore, is to establish a shortlist of suppliers to contact and it is worth spending some time on this. You should start by contacting a number of likely suppliers - manufacturers, software houses and bureaux as you feel appropriate. A basic checklist of the sort of questions to ask is given in Appendix 2. Inform each supplier that you are compiling a shortlist and do not wish for a quotation or even a visit yet. You might even use this stage to begin to determine whether or not your requirements can be met by a package program solution.

You should be sure to ask each prospective supplier for at least two references from customers already using his products in similar circumstances and call them to check on the quality of the work done and the supplier's ability to keep to costs and timescales. From this research it will be possible to shortlist the most promising suppliers who should then be sent the Requirements Specification. A date should be set for submission of the complete quotation - allow about four weeks - and each supplier should be informed that it is a competitive tender.

Despite your efforts to be concise and objective in the specification you will find that suppliers can place some obscure interpretations on requirements. Expect therefore to spend some time at this stage answering suppliers' queries to ensure each has a full understanding of your systems needs. It is essential to insist on written answers from them or write down any claims a supplier may make for future reference.

During discussions a supplier may give helpful advice or suggest alternative solutions. By all means adopt good ideas, but avoid leading him by giving different information from that in the specification. Otherwise, at the evaluation stage, you will not be able to make objective comparisons between the quotations received.

Evaluation

Once all the quotations have been received, comparison and evaluation can begin. One of the best ways to tackle this is to set out on a large sheet of analysis paper all the features offered and then mark them off by supplier. Some suggested headings are given in Appendix 3.

Once all the salient facts have been assimilated it should be possible to select the system which meets your requirements at the best price. The competitive tender approach often produces a wide range of solutions and prices. On the other hand, if the solutions are close in terms of features and price, this is the time to raise the question of discounts or special offers.

When the choice of supplier has been made, the preferred one should be asked for sample contracts. Letters of regret should not yet be sent to the unsuccessful contenders as you may not succeed in negotiating satisfactory terms with your preferred supplier. You may have to reach agreement with suppliers of hardware and software separately, although you should always attempt to make one supplier responsible for the entire project.

The Contract Stage

Negotiating the contracts

Negotiating the right contract terms is the most critical stage of the entire exercise. Until now possibilities have been explored and the choice narrowed but little if any money has been spent and no commitments have been entered into.

If now, having carefully chosen the best supplier and system for your needs, you do not ensure by negotiation that the contract with the supplier represents accurately the position you believe you have agreed, then the previous work will be largely wasted. Once the contract is signed there is no going back, so make sure that the terms are fair to both sides and that what you require of the system is clearly set out in the contract. Some suggestions for headings to consider in your negotiations are set out in Appendix 4.

Pressure will usually be brought to bear on you by the supplier at this stage to sign quickly. Incentives may be offered or the need to get everything running before a year end (yours or his) pointed out. But it is vital that the contract terms are first properly negotiated and this can take some considerable time.

This is also the time to have all the arguments. Once a contract has been signed and your business is dependent on the computer system, it is too late to wish that specific responsibilities and duties had been incorporated in the terms. Now is the moment also to recall all the reassurances which the supplier made during the quotation stage, and to insist that they are written into the contract if you consider them important.

Hardware manufacturers are usually unwilling to vary the terms of their standard contract significantly and may try a number of arguments to frustrate your demands. Software and systems houses are generally more amenable to negotiating terms. However, they tend to allow for this in advance by trying to weight their standard form of agreement heavily to their advantage.

You may well be wondering whether or not it really is possible to negotiate when simply purchasing an inexpensive microcomputer and some standard software packages. The answer is almost certainly that it is not. In circumstances where any custom-written programs are concerned, though, negotiation is essential, as you are endeavouring to buy a <u>solution to a business problem</u> rather than just equipment and programs.

The nature of computer agreements

When a business decides to enter into an agreement with a computer supplier, the relationship is usually sealed by the parties signing an order form for each major element of the agreement. Often there will be a separate agreement for hardware purchase, hardware hire, software and maintenance, even if they are only constituent parts of a complete system to be provided by the same supplier. If the system is complex and is to be installed in a number of stages, the customer may have to sign many forms; sometimes the same forms appear more than once.

The normal order form is invariably the supplier's own pre-printed document. The face tends to be a series of boxes or spaces for the information that will identify the nature of the agreement, its subject-matter, the parties and prices. The reverse of the form contains standard terms, which define the scope of the agreement, specify the responsibilities of the parties and legislate for specific occurrences; the print is usually small, like that of many commercial documents, while the provisions are expressed formally, sometimes using terms with specific legal significance. The content and wording of these standard terms differ considerably between computer suppliers.

Most computer agreement forms are contract documents, but some have other characteristics. The type of rules that apply to an agreement depend on the legal nature of the agreement. For example, software agreements usually take the form of licences; they have contractual characteristics but they also operate under the law relating to copyright. However, what matters from the practical business point of view is that the parties understand the commitments being made and that any formal documents they sign represent their mutual intentions completely and accurately.

The final agreement is more than a formal document which acts as the preliminary to installing a system. If sufficiently detailed, it should provide legal protection for both parties, but its real advantages are of greater practical importance, for it can:

(a) anticipate problems and define acceptable solutions;
(b) ensure that both parties have the same general and detailed objectives;
(c) motivate the parties to complete vital tasks.

Rather than being a document to be used in disputes or litigation, the agreement should help both to avoid problems and to give positive help to the parties in their joint undertaking. The final agreement is the vehicle for expressing the parties' understanding of each other's intentions and capabilities.

A good computer agreement has some of the characteristics of a business action plan with clear rules for achieving the plan's objectives and with contingency provisions to assist in the event of difficulties or failure. Most customers with little experience of computer systems will feel that, rather than just buying equipment or the right to use software, they are obtaining help, advice and the implementation of a complete working system. It is important therefore that the agreement reflects the dynamic nature of the relationship between supplier and customer.

The last paragraph indicates the true nature of computer agreements, many of which relate to the mutual development of a complete system. That system may, in some cases, require several years to complete.

To achieve a satisfactory position some amendment of the supplier's standard terms will often be needed, as well as the incorporation of new clauses covering special items. There will be a need to ensure that all the supplier's standard terms are checked, that you are prepared to accept them and that they do not conflict with the final document. It is not unknown for suppliers to make promises verbally or in letters which are then specifically excluded from the contract by a clause in their standard agreement which is there for precisely that purpose.

You may be asked to send a letter of intent, perhaps to obtain a level of discount allegedly shortly to be discontinued or possibly to ensure an earlier hardware delivery. Always make such letters subject to the formal contract. The aim is to make all the hardware and software elements of the agreement dependent on each other. This way, if the software is unsuitable, you will not be saddled with a computer you cannot use. If any of the supplier's terms are truly unacceptable, and his salesman, area manager or other negotiator cannot or will not amend them, then you may be forced to fall back on the runner-up in the quotations.

Finally, make sure to allow adequate time to read all the terms, obtain additional advice from computer specialists and a solicitor and resolve any queries before the date set for signature or expiry of the validity of the offer.

Buy, rent or lease?

There is no blanket answer to the question: 'Should we buy, rent or lease?' Factors which may influence the decision are those which affect the acquisition of any item of capital plant, e.g.

1. Does the company currently have the funds available for purchase?
2. How long will this computer meet your needs? Do you have confidence in the system volume projections?
3. Does the company have a need for the capital allowances?

Some suppliers offer an arrangement whereby a short-term rental can be converted into a purchase option with credit being given for a proportion of the rental paid. In this way outright purchase can be delayed until the customer has run the system for a while and has confidence that the equipment will meet requirements.

Do not be afraid to ask the prospective supplier to indicate alternative means of acquisition and what each would cost. It is also worth asking several independent leasing companies for comparative quotations if this seems a suitable method of financing for your particular circumstances.

System Implementation

At this point, with the contract signed, only the half-way stage of the computerisation exercise has been reached. So far the problem has been to reduce a large range of solution options to just one. Now begins the task of bringing the implementation phase to a successful conclusion.

More people may become active participants in the project at this stage. But even staff not directly affected will get to hear of plans and may worry about changes in jobs or even redundancy. Computers have a largely unmerited reputation for causing unemployment. It is therefore a good idea to make a point of telling everyone what is going to happen and why.

Planning

Implementation must be a joint exercise if it is to be successful. Unless both you and your supplier(s) together are totally committed to achieving a certain goal by a set date the project could become beset by difficulties. Each stage to be covered in the implementation should be set out in an action plan and a completion date allocated. Remember to allow time for changing clerical systems which may not be computerised but which may be affected, and be generous when allocating time for training and testing.

Typical stages in this part of the project might be:

1.	Hardware delivery lead time	Preparation of outline computer design
2.	Preparation of program specification	Programming
3.	Program testing	Clerical systems development
4.	Printing of special stationery	Planning system testing
5.	System testing	Correction of program 'bugs'
6.	Recruitment of staff	Training
7.	Documentation preparation	Taking on of static file data
8.	Take-over of dynamic file data	Parallel running
9.	Live running.	

Control and project management

Each computer implementation project must have a person or group from the user company responsible for the success of the venture. This responsibility should not be abdicated to the supplier, for an increasing problem, as hardware prices reduce, is that few suppliers can continue to afford to include much in the way of training and implementation support in the purchase price. At least, though, the supplier should nominate one person as the major contact who will be responsible for checking progress and quality of work done and reporting at any progress meetings. This is one of the areas of expertise to check when taking up references.

There is nothing esoteric in controlling computer projects. As with any other project there must be a procedure for achieving an organised development of several interrelated activities. The key factors in a normal project are:

(a) planning;
(b) working to the plan;
(c) monitoring performance;
(d) taking corrective action where necessary;
(e) amending the plan if necessary.

There should be regular meetings (kept deliberately brief) to review progress and take positive action to correct any deviation from the agreed plan. All parties to the project should be represented at progress meetings. For short projects regular meetings may be unnecessary and meetings on specific dates relating to the scheduled completion of key events (programming, documentation, system testing, etc.) can be used to monitor progress.

Conclusion

The advent of the microprocessor has had a profound effect upon computerised business systems, and microcomputers have replaced the use of a bureau as a company's first step into computing. To run most business applications, the computers must, as a minimum, have diskette storage and a printer, which means that the total cost including programs will be in the region of £5000 and not the £500 some advertisements would have us believe.

Decide what you want to do on the computer before you buy any equipment. Unless you are prepared to spend a great deal of time and effort doing your own programming, it is best to go to a systems company until the programs available in the High Street are in a better developed state.

If you go through all the steps described in Part II, you should ensure that you avoid purchasing a system that will be unable to do the job required of it. Installing the wrong system can have dire consequences for the first time user company. Whereas 15 years ago you needed to have a lot of money available to buy a computer and make such a mistake, you can now wreck your business systems for a relatively small sum!

Appendix 1
CHECKLIST OF CONTENTS FOR A SPECIFICATION

1. An outline description of the business, showing its locations and any plans for expansion. Attach an organisation chart showing departmental staff levels.
2. A broad description of what the computer is required to do.
    Include a flowchart illustrating the interaction of all the main systems.
3. For each system include:

    (a) a detailed flowchart showing the processing required;
    (b) sample of input documents (format and content);
    (c) a list of files to be held (contents and how you want to retrieve the information);
    (d) details of output needs (formats, contents, print or screen, frequencies);
    (e) special processing requirements calculations.

4. Current volumes of data (with peak loads) and growth expected.
5. Timing constraints (availability of data and minimum processing times possible). Response times to enquiries. Jobs to be operated concurrently.
6. Location constraints and description of the typical environment for the equipment.
7. Security and back-up requirements especially:

    (a) recovery procedures;
    (b) audit trail and system consistency and security checks.

8. Anything else which you feel is relevant.

Appendix 2
CHECKLIST OF INFORMATION REQUIRED FROM SHORTLISTED SUPPLIER

1. How long have they been in business and what is the history of their company's development?

2. Have they installed systems in your locality similar to the one you require. Can they give the names of two customers to whom you can speak directly?

3. Where are they based and how quickly can they respond to service calls? And would these promises be written into the contract?

4. What type of machine might they propose? How long has this been released and what is the minimum delivery lead time?

5. What is the approximate cost of an annual maintenance agreement?

6. Is ancillary equipment required (e.g. air conditioning or voltage regulators)?

7. How do they normally undertake a project to implement a computer system? What project management expertise do they have?

8. What training is provided? What is the approximate cost?

9. What documentation is provided and to what standard?

10. Will a warranty period be offered for software errors?

11. What are the additional costs for operating system software?

Appendix 3
EVALUATION CHECKLIST

1.   Number of their machines installed?

2.   Core (memory) size in bytes.   What user core is available?

3.   Number and size of disk drives.

4.   Number of VDUs and size of screens.

5.   Number of printers and print lines per minute.

6.   Maximum upgrade possible on this range of hardware.

7.   Core utilisation by operating system.

8.   Anticipated delivery lead times.

9.   Languages supported.

Software

10.   Package, conversion or custom written programs.

11.   Languages used.

12.   Number of programs.

13.   Scheduled development timescales.

Service

14.   Nearest service engineer's base.

15. Regular service downtime.

16. Minimum response time guaranteed.

17. Nearest similar machine for back-up.

Responsibility

18. How many suppliers will you have to deal with?

19. How many contracts?

Cost

20. Capital costs.

21. Annual costs on rental basis.

22. Annual costs on leased basis.

23. Costs of ancillary equipment and services.

24. Likely implementation costs.

Special features

25. Software utilities or other aids offered by the supplier.

Appendix 4.1
COMPUTER AGREEMENTS: GENERAL POINTS

The main general points to consider in computer agreements are:

1. Parties:

    (a) identify clearly;
    (b) should related customer organisations be included?
    (c) should related supplier organisations be included?

2. Subject matter:

    (a) describe exactly;
    (b) refer to supplier's proposals and literature.

3. Location: consider inclusion of alternative locations.

4. Price:

    (a) total price;
    (b) deposits and instalments;
    (c) discounts;
    (d) increases/price reviews;
    (e) currency;
    (f) price relationship with other customers;
    (g) attendance/time rates (for services);
    (h) ancillary costs (e.g. delivery).

5. Payment:

    (a) timing and dates;
    (b) consequences of late payment or non-payment.

6.   Delivery:

   (a)   responsibilities;
   (b)   physical arrangements;
   (c)   charges.

7.   Timing:

   (a)   specify target date and acceptable tolerances;
   (b)   relate to other key implementation dates.

8.   Duration and renewal (of limited period agreements).

9.   Performance standards:

   (a)   implementation standards and timing;
   (b)   skills, abilities and knowledge of supplier representatives.

10.   Staff recruitment: should the supplier be restricted?

11.   Formal communications:

   (a)   state method for transferring information/documents;
   (b)   form, method and representatives;
   (c)   explain each party's organisation structure.

12.   Customer's freedom: is future choice unduly restricted?

13.   Define technical and frequently used terms.

14.   Use:

   (a)   supplier should specify standards and requirements for using the subject matter;
   (b)   avoid restrictions on using other equipment, software and services.

15.   Limitations: consider whether user limitations, such as those relating to site, company or country, will affect possible business developments.

16.   Maintenance:

   (a)   normally, ensure that the supplier is responsible for maintenance;
   (b)   avoid conflict between maintenance provisions of different agreements;
   (c)   should not supplant replacement in cases of serious failure.

Appendix 4.2
COMPUTER AGREEMENTS: LEGAL POINTS

The main legal points to consider in computer agreements are:

1. Applicable law.

2. Parties:

    (a)   consider the effects of the delegated performance;
    (b)   consider the effects of the supplier's legal status changing (e.g. being taken over/being liquidated);
    (c)   review the parties' rights to assign.

3. Relationship of agreements:

    (a)   should a series of related agreements be linked?
    (b)   are there any inconsistencies between agreements?

4. Pre-agreement discussions:

    (a)   if fundamental, incorporate;
    (b)   consider especially the requirements' specification and the supplier's proposal;
    (c)   consider the effect of clauses rendering the final agreement definitive.

5. Representations:

    (a)   consider their relative importance;
    (b)   consider how to incorporate;
    (c)   document representations not incorporated.

6.   Status of terms:

   (a)   consider their relative importance and make this clear;
   (b)   consider the consequences of breach and clarify;
   (c)   state any right to damages;
   (d)   state the right to other specified benefits.

7.   Breach procedure:

   (a)   specify the procedure;
   (b)   include a method of notification and rectification period.

8.   Exclusion clauses:

   (a)   effect is reduced by statutory and common-law limitations;
   (b)   but review them carefully.

9.   Relative rights and liabilities; the customer should be in no worse a position than the supplier.

10.   Remedies: specify wherever possible, particularly in relation to key aspects of the system or key implementation stages.

11.   Disputes:

   (a)   specify a procedure to avoid unnecessary litigation;
   (b)   consider both informal procedures and arbitration.

12.   Formal communications: give legal recognition to a formal communications procedure.

13.   Variation: consider whether a method should be specified.

14.   Intellectual property (patents/copyrights/trademarks/trade secrets). Consider:

   (a)   the extent of the supplier's rights and undertakings as to their existence;
   (b)   the rights that are, and can be, extended to the customer;
   (c)   royalties, including the acts that will incur liability and the right to repayment if rights are not granted lawfully;
   (d)   compensation for infringing others' rights.

15.   Confidentiality:

   (a)   consider imposing on the supplier a duty not to reveal information about the customer and his business;
   (b)   consider the effects of the supplier imposing such a duty, particularly in connection with consulting professional advisers.

Appendix 4.3
COMPUTER AGREEMENTS: HARDWARE PURCHASE

The main points to consider in hardware purchase agreements are:

1. Identification:

    (a) identify accurately;
    (b) describe capabilities.

2. Capacity and performance should be related to:

    (a) other hardware being supplied;
    (b) operating and applications software it is to support;
    (c) transaction data volumes, including peaks;
    (d) type and frequency of outputs;
    (e) terminal usage;
    (f) processing time available.

3. Suitability and quality: consider whether the supplier should undertake that the hardware is appropriate for clearly specified applications and that it will meet certain reliability criteria.

4. Replacement:

    (a) define when equipment should be replaced;
    (b) consider replacement at different levels - components/sub-assemblies/complete items/the total configuration;
    (c) consider the possibility of changes if replacement impracticable.

5. Compatibility: should the supplier warrant compatibility with other equipment?

6. Installation and commissioning:

   (a)   specify timing, responsibilities and payment;
   (b)   define tests and yardsticks;
   (c)   specify responsibilities and location;
   (d)   define method for recording test completion.

7. Standby:

   (a)   are standby facilities necessary?
   (b)   should the supplier provide them?
   (c)   define possible standby facilities;
   (d)   define applicable circumstances and commencement procedures.

8. Physical requirements: the supplier should specify physical and environmental requirements.

9. Improvements:

   (a)   should a development path be guaranteed?
   (b)   consider whether trade-in credits are required.

Appendix 4.4
COMPUTER AGREEMENTS: SOFTWARE LICENCES

Software means the programs that are used to instruct a computer to perform intended tasks. It can include programs that allow the computer to function 'intelligently' and those that actually perform the required tasks.

Software can be bought or hired, but it is much more common for it to be the subject of a licence, to which the following points mainly relate:

1. Determine whether the agreement relates to a licence, sale or lease.

2. State the licence period and:

   (a) provide for termination;
   (b) link the period and termination to the use of related hardware and software;
   (c) consider likely developments in the type of software;
   (d) consider possible changes in the organisation's systems;
   (e) consider whether the supplier is also the hardware supplier.

3. Charges are covered under hardware hire. In addition:

   (a) there should be no charge for security/standby copies;
   (b) additional copies should be provided on favourable terms.

4. Identification and capabilities:

(a) identify each program exactly, describing its functions;
(b) consider incorporating in the agreement documentation for complex or critical programs;
(c) define the memory and processing implications of all software;
(d) incorporate guarantees of suitability and quality;
(e) state that the programs should perform in accordance with the supplier's documentation and representations;
(f) guarantee compatibility with hardware and related software.

5. Enhancements and developments:

(a) specify the version to which the licence relates;
(b) state the supplier's responsibility for providing new versions;
(c) avoid differences between the versions covered by different agreements.

6. Support and error correction:

(a) establish responsibility to correct errors free of charge;
(b) serious continuing errors should lead to complete replacement;
(c) define level of support, including assistance with problems;
(d) protect against support failure (make program source codes available).

7. Documentation:

(a) right to up-to-date practical explanations for each new version;
(b) right should run with the licence.

8. Acceptance testing:

(a) establish standards and a suitable programme for testing;
(b) specify the aims of testing and acceptance/rejection criteria.

9. Custom-written software:

(a) obtain exclusive rights, preventing the supplier from using it except under licence;
(b) for amendments to standard software, joint rights may have to suffice.

Appendix 4.5
COMPUTER AGREEMENTS: MAINTENANCE

Maintenance agreements normally relate to hardware, but software is also suitable subject matter. Occasionally the same agreement may provide for the maintenance of both hardware and software. The following, which are the main points, apply equally to both:

1. Nature:

    (a)   specify whether the service is preventive, remedial or both;
    (b)   in choosing the service, ascertain the importance of the system and the vulnerability of the business;
    (c)   detail the service, preferably in relation to the difficulties envisaged.

2. Applicability:

    (a)   maintenance should not restrict the supplier's other duties to rectify inadequacies;
    (b)   it should not prevent essential replacement of equipment or components.

3. Standard of performance:

    (a)   specify the level of skill and competence required;
    (b)   state the criteria for taking each type of remedy;
    (c)   establish criteria for attributing breakdown/malfunction to inadequate maintenance;
    (d)   state the rules for maintenance visits.

4. The period should be related to the subject-matter's life:

    (a)   if hired/licensed, the maintenance period should correspond;
    (b)   if purchased, maintenance should run with its useful life;
    (c)   should cessation of maintenance be grounds for rescission/termination of main agreement?

5. Price:

    (a)   terms to be reasonable and no worse than for other customers;
    (b)   relate increases to published price lists;
    (c)   retain right to terminate for unreasonable price increases;
    (d)   no charge for fulfilling other responsibilities under maintenance guise.

6. Procedures to be established for:

    (a)   customer requests for visits;
    (b)   supplier notification of routine visits.

7. Compatibility:

    (a)   maintenance not to change the main subject matter fundamentally;
    (b)   if the subject matter is changed, then, if changed by the supplier, he should not be able to rely on it in the event of breach;
    (c)   if subject matter is changed by a non-supplier, damages should be payable.

8. Rebates:

    (a)   maintenance rebates if subject matter unusable for a noticeable period;
    (b)   hire/licence rebates if supplier maintenance responsible for subject-matter failure.

Appendix 4.6
COMPUTER AGREEMENTS: SERVICES

Many organisations in the computer industry provide services and assistance to existing or potential users. These may be intangible, as in the case of advice and training; they may lead to something more specifically linked with a computer system, such as the writing of software. Many agreements for the provision of hardware and software often include, or refer to, the provision of supporting services; a common example is maintenance, which is a type of service. Some agreements are limited wholly to the provision of services, the most frequently encountered example being the writing of programs.

Some points to be considered are:

1. Establish nature of subject matter:

    (a) is the aim to achieve an end result or to provide supplier's time?
    (b) will any means of fulfilling the contract suffice?

2. Define the subject matter carefully.

3. Price:

    (a) relate to work to be performed;
    (b) where service is time-based, provide a clear formula.

4. Payment:

    (a) relate to stages of performance;
    (b) link with achievement of specified standards.

5. Timing:

    (a)   establish maximum length of a time-based service;
    (b)   state the latest completion date.

6. Establish standards for the end-result by relating it to:

    (a)   its purpose;
    (b)   how it will be used;
    (c)   the system with which it may be used;
    (d)   a measure of effectiveness.

7. Rectification of errors/inadequacies:

    (a)   for software, see Appendix 4.4;
    (b)   for other services, specify responsibility for continued support;
    (c)   specify whether free of charge/rate to be charged;
    (d)   specify damages for very poor performance;
    (e)   provide for good documentation to assist rectification by others.

8. Working arrangements:

    (a)   facilities required;
    (b)   attendance times;
    (c)   certification of attendance;
    (d)   provision of assistance.

9. Acceptance tests for custom-written software should normally be more stringent than those for standard program packages.

10. Provide for termination in case of failure to satisfy essential requirements:

    (a)   quality of service;
    (b)   slowness of execution;
    (c)   poor documentation.

11. Skill and knowledge requirements:

    (a)   should be fundamental terms;
    (b)   right to veto/endorse staff.

Index